Routledge Revivals

Auguste Comte

First published in 1928, *Auguste Comte* is a biography of the famous French philosopher Auguste Comte, the founder of the doctrine of positivism. In this book, the author traces Comte's journey from his birth till his death. The final chapter 'After Days' provides a commentary on the changes the society underwent over a course of seventy years after Comte's death. The author draws upon the works of Auguste Comte published during the period 1829–1927 to give an extensive and well researched account of the philosopher's life and work.

Auguste Comte

Thinker and Lover

Jane M. Style

Routledge Revivals
Routledge
Taylor & Francis Group

First published in 1928
by Kegan Paul, Trench Trubner & Co., Ltd.

This edition first published in 2025 by Routledge
4 Park Square, Milton Park, Abingdon, Oxon, OX14 4RN

and by Routledge
605 Third Avenue, New York, NY 10017

Routledge is an imprint of the Taylor & Francis Group, an informa business

Publisher's Note
The publisher has gone to great lengths to ensure the quality of this reprint but points out that some imperfections in the original copies may be apparent.

Disclaimer
The publisher has made every effort to trace copyright holders and welcomes correspondence from those they have been unable to contact.

A Library of Congress record exists under LCCN: 29005094

ISBN: 978-1-032-90747-5 (hbk)
ISBN: 978-1-003-55960-3 (ebk)
ISBN: 978-1-032-90748-2 (pbk)

Book DOI 10.4324/9781003559603

ORDER
LOVE
PROGRESS
AUGUSTE COMTE 1798-1857
CLOTILDE DE VAUX 1815-1846

AUGUSTE COMTE

THINKER AND LOVER

BY

JANE M. STYLE

Author of *War! Its Cause and Prevention*
And *The Voice of the 19th Century: a Woman's Echo*

LONDON
KEGAN PAUL, TRENCH TRUBNER & CO., LTD.
BROADWAY HOUSE: 68-74 CARTER LANE, E.C.
1928

TO

S. S.

in gratitude for constant encouragement,

help and sympathy,

and

in memory of

JOHN KELLS INGRAM

and the task he laid upon me.

CONTENTS

AUGUSTE COMTE

THINKER AND LOVER

CHAPTER I

THE CHILD AND HIS MOTHER

IN 1797 there lived at Montpellier, in the South of France, a young merchant, Louis Comte, who had lately had the good fortune to win a beautiful and loving hearted woman and to bring her home as his wife.

Rosalie Boyer, who had become Madame Comte before our narrative begins, was of a deeply religious nature, an ardent Catholic and Royalist. It was nine years after the fall of the Bastille and France was passing through a stage of re-action; the bright hopes of the dawn of a new era for mankind had been dimmed by the outbreak of cruelty, torrents of blood had been shed as a result of the stimulation of the destructive instinct which so often takes place in times of excitement.

The hopes of the Catholics and Royalists were high that the moment was at hand when the altar and the throne would be re-established. The year before De Maistre had made his famous prophecy that there would either be a wonderful resusitation of Christianity or that a new religion would appear. " We are approaching ", he said, " the greatest of religious epochs ".

It may have been that echoes of this prophecy had reached Montpellier, that some of the preachers had tried to rouse the enthusiasm of their audiences and stimulate them to the work needed. Louis Comte, however, kind husband, honest merchant, and faithful Catholic, as he was, was no enthusiast; he was contented to do his work well and pray for the welfare of his Church and country, but the heart of Rosalie was a shrine where pure thoughts and earnest hopes were united and these were now concentrated on the child who was to be born; he would follow in the steps of the Catholic saints and help to restore the Church, and of the patriots who had redeemed their land from oppression. For Rosalie there could be no idea of a " new religion "; for her there was, or could be, only one, the Holy Catholic Faith, and she had no doubt that her child would be a devout son of the Catholic Church.

The old legends in which the mothers of redeemers or demigods had visions before their birth of the wonders their children were to perform may perhaps be explained by the effect upon the child of pre-natal conditions. In truth, the soul of the mother is as surely creating the soul of the child as her body is creating its body, and thus the earnest religious soul of Rosalie was reflected in her son although his opinions differed so widely from her own.

Her son was born on the 19th January, 1798.

There is a picture at Rio de Janeiro in which she is shown presenting him before the Catholic altar and dedicating him as, it is said, in the old legend, Hannah did the prophet Samuel. This picture is an idealisation of the artist but we know she did dedicate him in her heart and she named him after three saints of the Catholic Church: Isidore—Auguste—François Xavier, and after Mary the Mother of God. For nine years the child grew up by his mother's side, with a sister and brother who were born later,and under the care of the father, and these were the happiest years of Rosalie's life. With all her beloved ones around her she was able to spend herself in their service; this was, as her life and letters clearly shew, her highest idea of happiness.

Isidore, as he was then called, or Auguste, as he is known to the world, was of an ardent affectionate nature and between him and his mother there was a harmony of temperament. From her he learnt to worship the Virgin, the Saints, and the Trinity. With all a child's wondering veneration and unquestioning faith he knelt by her side and lavished upon that sweet and loving mother the treasure of his childish affection. Many years later, when a noble love had enlightened him as to the true values of life, he realised all that this early training had meant with its revelation of love and faith.

And she, watching over her child and appreciating his marvellous mental power, felt sure that her hopes for his future would be fulfilled, that he would be the chosen vessel who should raise the altar that had been cast down, and establish the throne in righteousness.

The father and mother consulting together were almost terrified at the intellectual development of the boy. Not feeling able to deal with it themselves they sought a tutor who prepared him for the Lycée. This tutor was old, and Auguste, in his eager desire for learning, often arrived with his books in the morning before the old man was up.

When Auguste was nine years old this happy time came to an end, it was decided that he should go as a boarder to the Lycée at Montpellier, and from that day he never again lived at home for any length of time. There is no written record of these nine years but the strength of the attachment between mother and son can be gathered from her letters and his later writings. He was her " well beloved ", her " adored son "; to think of him out of health and far from her was " heartbreaking "; " must we be always separated ", she writes, " What a painful existence!" And in his later writings Comte bitterly regrets that he was torn from her care so young. He had an extraordinary capacity for tenderness and this was now repressed and stunted until middle life. This repression, as is so often the case, re-acted disastrously on his conduct. The bad effect on his development was very present to him and in his ideal of the education of the future, the young boy is not to be sent away to conventual establishments, but to share in domestic life while his education is carried on. He was of course also separated from the rest of his family, from the control of his father (now appointed cashier at the tax office) and the pleasant companionship of sister and brother. It is doubtful whether his sister Alix would ever have helped him much in later life, for, such record as we have of her shews her as of a narrow outlook and quite lacking the tenderness of her mother Rosalie, but Adolphe, the youngest of the three, must have been of a noble nature, he describes in a letter, written to his brother when he was eighteen years of age, how he had been carried away by the idea of military glory, but, on comparing the career of a soldier with that of a doctor, he says that "one makes the misery of men and the other succours the unhappy." Shortly after, Adolphe died, and more than twenty years later, Comte, in writing to John Stuart Mill, speaks of having unfortunately lost the brother on whom he counted for fraternal intercourse.

Auguste went to the Lycée and although he had received only a few lessons from the old tutor he rapidly advanced in the school, distinguishing himself in every subject. He was small, delicate and undersized, but of an extraordinary courage, both physical and moral. As a little boy at school his moral courage was shown when before the whole class he expressed his hopes that the Spaniards would be successful in expelling Bonaparte from their country, and later, his physical courage, by his heroic endurance of an operation for the removal of a tumour during which he neither moved nor uttered a sound.

Before he was thirteen he had absorbed all the

teaching which was given on the literary side in the schools of public instruction, and the Director persuaded his father to let him begin mathematics. In this study he made such progress that at sixteen he gained one of the first places in the examinations for admission to the Polytechnic School of Paris, but could not be admitted for a year as he was too young.

His mathematical master was Daniel Encontre, for whose method of teaching, and social and philosophic outlook, he had the deepest veneration, expressed in the Dedication to his last work, " The Subjective Synthesis ". Encontre was delicate, and on one occasion when he was ill Auguste took his place and lectured with great success to his fellow students, standing on a chair to do so because of his short stature.

Thrown as Comte was on his own resources, so young and with his keen and powerful intellect, it was inevitable that he should lose faith in the religion his mother had taught him, and he tells us that when he was thirteen he had given up all faith in any outside power, had lost his royalist sympathies and become an ardent republican. Unfortunately, with the beliefs, which he was sure to lose, was bound up much of the moral training he had received and this resulted in unregulated conduct on his part. Most docile in learning, revering those who taught him, and with a friendly fraternal feeling for his fellow pupils, he was very rebellious when tyranny was shown, and was constantly in trouble because of his outspoken opposition to the powers that be.

His fellow pupils admired his great gifts and spoke of his prodigious memory; he could repeat a page which he had only read once.

We are not told at what moment his mother realised that he had fallen away from the belief which contained for her the only salvation, he was so candid and open hearted that it could not long have been concealed from her. We know how she wept and prayed for him through all the years of her life, wept and prayed and loved with no less fervour than Monica for her son Saint Augustine, but her fate was less happy because when Monica lived Catholicism was the force which was moving the west and attracting the vigorous intellects of the day, but when Rosalie strove for her son its power was passing, the new religion was about to dawn on the world. This was sad for her, but, for her son the consequent loss of belief in the moral sanctions was for a time disastrous, and very nearly wrecked his life and work.

Many youths were suffering from moral and mental scepticism, for the women were clinging to the old Catholic faith while the intellect of the time had cast it off and the mothers lost their hold on their sons at an early age.

In October, 1814, when he was sixteen and a half, Comte went to the Polytechnic at Paris. This celebrated school had been founded by the National Convention and was carried on in an ancient monastery not far from the Panthéon by the most learned men of France. The revolutionary spirit, which was its tradition, was still strong in the school in spite of the military discipline Bonaparte had instituted. Comte and his fellows strenuously opposed this military discipline, especially their being subjected to barrack life. The boy had already judged Bonaparte; it has been told how at ten years of age he objected to his aggression in Spain. Now he saw how by his constant wars he had established tyranny within the Empire and had arrayed all Europe against it without. Such was the judgment of Comte the boy and in later years he speaks of him as " the one who organised in the most disastrous way the worst political retrogression under which Humanity had ever sighed ".

Owing, however, to the way in which the Allies had treated France after they had banished Bonaparte to Elba, he was welcomed as a deliverer when he escaped, and his promises of reform believed. Comte and the other scholars prayed to be allowed to help in freeing their country, and they were drilled and prepared for this purpose. Bonaparte had no chance of carrying out his promises, of showing whether the leopard had indeed changed his spots, for he was quickly overthrown and Louis XVIII installed.

The Republican influence of the Polytechnic stimulated the philosophic and social direction Comte's genius had already taken. Here he met many eminent men, and youths who later became eminent; Poinsot was his mathematical master and under him he made rapid progress. The youngest in the school, and still childish looking and delicate, his fellow students said of him that he had the mind of a mature man, they called him " The Thinker ". He learnt so quickly that he had plenty of time for private reading. He studied the republican institutions of Europe and America, he compared modern and ancient times, striving to see the law of development; for, already the desire for universal regeneration was strong in his soul, and his constructive genius was so vigorous that almost as soon as he had lost his belief in theology he strove to find the foundation of a new faith.

From his earliest youth he had noticed that the belief in one God, which men had hoped would unite all, had resulted in dividing the Western world between two opposing monotheisms, while the truths of science were gradually uniting all. He concluded that the vague unreality of the theological beliefs could not unite men and his hope turned to science, for he felt that if the scientific method, which gained universal assent and led to rational prevision in the lower sciences, could be applied to social and political questions, uncertainty and revolution would be at an end. Therefore, he strove earnestly to prepare himself by continuous study.

His career at the Polytechnic came to an abrupt end, for when on one occasion a master shewed disrespect to the pupils Comte wrote a letter to him, which all signed, requesting him to resign. The school was already " suspect " by the Government because of its republican sympathies, the opportunity was seized to close it for a time and the young Comte was sent back to Montpellier under police supervision.

The distress and the disappointment of his parents

can be imagined. The Government appointments were generally given to the pupils of the Polytechnic and Comte, as one of the ablest, would have stood a good chance of an excellent position. Now the prospect was lost and he was thrown back on his own resources. It was impossible for his parents to understand him or his aims. His passion for spiritual liberty, as a necessary condition of social regeneration, must have seemed mere rebellion to them and must have wrung the devout and submissive heart of Rosalie. This passion was shewn in his delight in the promised freedom of the Press in 1815 and, in the same year, when his friend Valat, still a pupil at the Lycée of Montpellier, told him as a joke that they were given tickets to go to confession he answered finely that, far from making him laugh, it filled him with indignation:

> "Poor France!" he cries, "unhappy friends of Liberty. The noble efforts you made, at the peril of your lives to give your fellow citizens the possession of their rights are rendered useless and perhaps you will die the victims of your devotion to the cause of reason and Humanity" !

It is thus that the boy of seventeen writes to his schoolmate. We owe it to the faithful friendship of these two boys, whose correspondence was continued through many years, that much of the life of Comte is known to us.

He remained at home for a few months attending the lectures at the celebrated medical school of

Montpellier. Once more Rosalie had this beloved son beneath her roof and this would have been happiness to her but it was dimmed by the fact that their outlook on life was different.

He was bent on returning to Paris for he was already convinced of his mission. The suffering of the people and the disorder of society had touched his heart, he saw the need for reorganisation and felt that he must help in this supreme work. Paris was the centre of thought, there he could find the books he must study and could associate with the men who could inspire and help him. He must be about Humanity's business, the sorrowing of his parents could not hold him back. They did sorrow, his father only saw that he wanted to go penniless to Paris and would be an expense to him, his mother felt that she would lose him, and also dreaded the temptations of Paris for one of his ardent temperament. All three had formed a correct judgment. Auguste was often an expense to his father and never, even in the best of times, made much more than a bare subsistence; his life and work did lead him far away from his mother's hopes, and the result of the temptations of Paris nearly wrecked his career, but he did discover and put before the world the regenerating doctrine, and is widely recognised to-day as one of the greatest of the sons of men.

CHAPTER II

Under the Banyan Tree

ARRIVED in Paris, Comte began the concentrated study and meditation which was necessary to attain the results he expected. Poinsot, the eminent geometer, had by no means forgotten his brilliant pupil and helped him to find work in teaching mathematics, which enabled him to live. Just to live was all he cared for, every moment that could be spared from the necessary lessons was given to study and meditation. Hour after hour he would remain plunged in thought sometimes prolonged through the night. On one occasion, during the conception of the "Philosophy", his thought was maintained for eighty hours. This youth, not yet twenty, recalls the legend of the Buddha under the banyan tree, when he also was meditating how to regenerate the life of man.

He saw how the luminous ideas which had inspired the French revolution had apparently passed away, and how its later phases, and the wars of the Empire, had alienated Europe and turned men back to retrograde beliefs.

He carefully studied the writers of the 18th century; Fontenelle who helped him to his discovery of relativity, Maupertuis whose works on the progress of science and origin of language were of deep interest, Montesquieu whose conception of law and a social organism approached very near to his own, Adam Smith whose masterly use of the historic method in his enquiries into economic and moral questions won his admiration, Fréret who used the scientific method in his historic research, Duclos, the witty writer, whose observations on character are material for positive morals, and who defines virtue as " an effort over self in favour of others ". Turgot, who vaguely foresaw the " Law of the Three Stages " and whose wise administration and enlightened philanthropy almost prevented the Revolution, Diderot, the encyclopedic thinker who, had the time been ripe, might have been the founder of the Positive Philosophy, and Hume who was indeed largely its founder.

Comte also studied De Maistre, whose work on the Pope enabled him to avoid the error of the eighteenth century thinkers and to appreciate the Middle Ages.

Had he needed more inspiration he would have found it in the condition of Paris at this time. In a letter to Valat he speaks of the misery of the people who were starving, and with indignation of the luxurious life of others, the dances, the extravagance and the ostentation. How greatly the social regeneration was needed!

He " plunged in thought again " and soon made

his first important discovery. The space in which we see abstract forms and which had been considered the most distant objective existence, was not objective at all, but subjective, created by the mind of man. This conception, which Condorcet had not reached but which Kant had foreshadowed, was intimately connected with his second discovery of relativity.

The statement of this truth: " Tout est relatif; violà la seule chose absolue " is found in a publication called " L'Industrie ", which appeared at the end of September, 1817, and marked the complete *revolution* in the human outlook: the absolute truth was no more to be looked for, all had to be considered in relation to time and place. This was a necessary condition of bringing scientific observation to bear on history and was the preparation for the science of sociology of which Comte was to become the founder. The important work of Einstein, a hundred years later, was an illustration in science of this philosophic truth. Comte had pointed out that the "Law of gravitation" might be superseded by further knowledge. Yet how slow the world has been in comprehending all the bearings of Comte's discovery.

About this time Comte came into contact with St. Simon in whom he thought he had found the successor of the 18th century thinkers and, won by the charm and apparent sincerity of this popular idol, he devoted himself to him with enthusiastic veneration. It was an unfortunate acquaintance, for it drew his attention away, for a time, from the construction of positive philosophy to political action, it led him into premature writing and, for the moment, stimulated the desire of immediate fame and prosperity.

Comte has himself selected from his writings of this period the sentences which were of permanent value. One was the truth quoted above; another : "The liberty of the press gives a consultative authority to all citizens". This connection with St. Simon could not last long for the disciple was so much greater than the master that, as his thought developed, he found out the fallacies and shallowness of the man he had regarded as a great thinker. The reputation of St. Simon gradually declined while that of Comte became one of the

> "Immortal lights
> That rise up slowly in the sky
> And shine there everlastingly."

By 1824 all connection between them had ceased.

At this period of Comte's life, his neglect of his mother is much to be regretted, she was wearing her heart out in anxiety for him at Montpellier. He wrote seldom and in the letters from home there is a constant cry for more frequent news. The father tells him how his mother, suffering from nervous fever, recovered at once on receiving a letter from him, and she speaks of her suffering while waiting for letters. Probably the cause was not only his concentration on his work but the difficulty of telling her of his life; the work that absorbed him, had she understood it, would have filled her with grief, and in his private life, as we shall see presently, he knew he was neglecting the precepts of his childhood.

How could he write to her of these things! They had no mutual acquaintances about whom he could have told her details; it was not possible for his sincere nature to make anything up. The utmost he could do was to conceal, and his letters to Valat shew his anxiety that his parents shall not hear things that would hurt them, such as his relationship with St. Simon. Like so many men in early youth he was not fully alive to the meaning of a mother's love and suffering, and in his lonely life there were none of the daily acts of kindness which develop tenderness and consideration for others.

But his absorption in the social purpose of his life never failed, and in 1818, in a letter to Valat, speaking of standing armies, he says:

> "The thorough examination that I have so far been able to give to politics has convinced me that this institution is, to-day, the only obstacle to social organisation from whatever point of view it be regarded."

He points out that a standing army is not suitable for defence, and instances the wars in America, Spain, Germany and France, which were all won by the armed citizens under the names of Guerillas, Landwehr, Landsturm and Carmagnoles. The perpetual peace proposed by Henri IV and Sully cannot be brought about by kings, for "Royalty", he says, "has been from the beginning an essentially military affair", and even in England has lost it very incompletely; for peace to come about, the people must have a voice in the State.

In 1819 there are expressions of the deep social feeling by which he was inspired and of the clear thought which he brought to bear upon social life. Valat had written that he wished to live in the country, Comte answers that he also hoped some day to do so and, if he consulted his own taste only, should agree with him entirely, but he asks whether there was not some selfishness in the thought and points out that to live for men is also necessary for happiness. He writes:

> "My friend, this hard-working open-hearted and worthy class of men that we both love is oppressed, it is basely robbed by its superiors who nevertheless profit entirely by the fruit of its labours. That it may no longer minister to the infamous luxury and base idleness of its masters, that the social order organised to-day for the benefit of useless people may become organised for the useful, there my friend is a duty for us, for us who have come from the oppressed classes and may by our education and our gifts do something to bring about this great change. A number of capable men, allowing themselves to be led away by the temptations of wealth and power, place themselves under the banner of the oppressors, others, more honest, who will not do this, are yet content to be peaceable spectators of the struggle. But who then will be on the side of the weak? You my friend you will join, we will join, a small number of enlightened men who will

> work openly to free the many from the tyranny and pillage of the few, you will not be content to be neutral you will give your help to the general cause. In times less fortunate than ours those who had clearly seen the sad lot of the working classes might limit themselves to declining to share the plunder, being persuaded of the impossibility of making the slightest effort for the workers against the idle, but to-day it is not so, thanks to the progress of knowledge and of civilisation that which was formerly but a dream can begin to be realised, war, luxury, poverty, legal and organised plunder can disappear gradually. It is possible by gentle and easy methods to establish peace firmly and to bring comfort to the mass of the people ".

In an essay " The Separation of Opinions and Aspirations " he points out that the mass of the people have the aspirations, they know the need and must say what they would have, it is for the rulers to carry out their wishes. But between the two there must be the skilled men who will say how this is to be done. Special knowledge and skill is needed here even more than in physical, chemical, or medical sciences where the need of skilled men is considered unquestionable.

These men would form the Spiritual Power, which he wanted to see established, with philosophic outlook above the specialist men of science of whatever department of knowledge.

It has been said, by many who were deeply interested in Comte's method of dealing with science but had no wish to see it carried on to the reorganisation of society, that the latter part of his life and work were out of harmony with the earlier part, but his earliest inspiration was concerned with the reorganisation of life and the replacing of the old by the new Spiritual Power, in fact his first idea was that this could be brought about directly, was only after further consideration that he saw that the whole knowledge of the past must be understood and science carried into social matters before this could be accomplished; his devoted labours of more than twelve years were deliberately undertaken as foundation for the supreme task of his life.

In 1820 he wrote the essay, " A Brief Estimate of Modern History ", in which he traced the double movement, the gradual decline of the theologico-military system and the growth of the positive or pacific-industrial state. He also shewed the contrast between France and England as the central or local power prevailed.

The appointment of Poinsot, as a member of the Committee of Instruction, gave Comte hope that he would get some public post as teacher of mathematics which would make his livelihood less precarious. Whilst preparing himself for the scientific work he hoped to do he attended a course of lectures on astronomy by Delambre. They were mutually attracted and the old man took the youth to his home to continue his instruction.

In 1822, when he was in his 25th year, Comte wrote the essay, " Plan of the Scientific Operations Necessary for Re-organising Society ", which was a remarkable forecast of the whole of his life's work and shews an almost incredible width of view and intellectual power in so young a man.

Only in two points it did not attain the reality and completeness of his mature work; he had not yet disentangled the science of morals from sociology, and he attributed to intellectual energy the advance which further experience convinced him was the result of social feeling.

The heads of this essay will show the task he had marked out for himself.

In the introduction he reviews the condition of modern society, shewing the mistakes that kings (or rulers) and the people had made in attempting to end the Revolution; the rulers trying to restore the past order, and the people depending on the critical or destructive method, he points out that the only escape from these mistakes will be found in the formation of an organic doctrine which will convince both:

> " The destination of society, now come to maturity, is neither to inhabit for ever the old and miserable hut which its infancy erected, as kings suppose, nor to live eternally without shelter after having left it, as the people imagined. Its destiny is rather this, that, aided by acquired experience, it should with all the accumulated materials, construct an

edifice fitted for its needs and enjoyment. Such is the noble enterprise reserved for the present generation ".

The re-organisation of society requires two parts: the theoretical, or spiritual, aims at developing the plan, the practical, or temporal, develops the means. The plan necessarily comes first. Modern society, as opposed to ancient, is industrial rather than military, but, because this aim has never been clearly expressed, our action is confused between the two, and certainly is not definitely pointed to the industrial. The division between the Spiritual and the Temporal Power is then necessary. The decline of Catholicism must not destroy this:

> " It is evident that it ought to be preserved with all the other conquests made by the human mind under the influence of the old regime, and which cannot perish with it ".

The Spiritual Power must be formed from men of science who will in this way unite Europe by offering to all a share in the re-organisation. They must raise politics into a science. By the nature of the human mind every branch of our knowledge must pass through three stages: fictitious, abstract and positive.

This is the celebrated "Law of the Three Stages", the law of mental evolution by which Comte founded social dynamics and made the scientific study of history possible. This law he discovered one morning after a night of profound meditation. His hierarchy of the sciences follows the law of the three stages, for man's conceptions pass through the three stages in the order of their complication, the simplest first on which the others rest, thus the examination of the period in which each science became positive or scientific gives it its place in the scale: mathematics, astronomy, physics, chemistry, biology, sociology. Before sociology could be founded it was necessary that the simpler sciences should have reached that stage. This condition was now fulfilled, for " politics ", he says, " have passed through the two first stages and are now ready for the third ". The divine right of kings was the theological, and the sovereignty of the people the metaphysical stage. The social state is the consequence of man's organisation and position in the scale of animals. It is not capable of explanation but its first object is to develop the tendency of man to act on the earth for his own advantage. To understand it, each epoch of the past must be examined to see how far advance towards perfection was possible in that time and place.

He called upon the learned men of Europe to devote themselves to the unification of knowledge and its dedication to social re-organisation, first to form a system of historic observations on the advance of the human mind, then to institute positive education so that the agents might be duly prepared, and, finally, to show the collective effect man could have on his surroundings. Politics can only become a science when it is recognised that social organisation depends on the civilisation of the time and that civilisation is subject to law. It is not enough to examine the present; the philosophic order is past, future, present, for, from the past, the future is deduced and then the action in the present can be wisely undertaken.

The thinkers are to make plans, the artists to idealise and incline men's minds to them, and the practical men to carry them out.

All positive science has foresight as its aim, and observation of the past will unveil the future in politics as it has in physics, chemistry and physiology, thus violent perturbations and revolutions will be avoided. He then reviews the attempts of his predecessors giving honour to Montesquieu, Condorcet and Cabanis; Condorcet he claims as his spiritual father.

This essay made Comte famous among the learned men of France and even in other countries. No one seems to have been sufficiently advanced to observe the error in reasoning which he was destined to correct in later years.

And yet, while he was describing the intellect as the driving force, he was himself an instance of the supreme force of feeling. It was his social feeling, his intense desire to help mankind, which was impelling him as we see by his own words to Tabarié at this time. He tells this friend that his family have heard of his success and are rejoicing that now he will become rich and famous, but he knows better, the work to which he has dedicated his life is more likely to lead to persecution, fame it may bring indeed but never daily bread. It is true that social feeling without his power of intellect would have been insufficient, but, without the social feeling, how soon personal desires, the persuasions of his friends and, later, a more intimate persecution to which he was to be subjected, would have led him to give his intellectual powers to work which would have given him immediate fame and put him at the head of the men of intellect of his day.

Since his time an enormous amount of material has been accumulated for social science but the thinkers of Europe have not yet responded to his call, though it rang in their ears a hundred years ago. He pointed out that the University in France in his time was quite incapable of conducting this synthetic change; its professors were specialists and literary men.

Our own English universities are to-day at about the same stage. Oxford, indeed, still attempts a synthesis, but it is by keeping to the old theological interpretations. The universities in our industrial centres are little more than superior technical schools carrying on useful special research in an admirable manner but making little attempt to unite their teaching into a whole, each subject remaining as almost a watertight compartment, the professors often knowing little of one another, and the Head chosen, no doubt for some good reason, but not for his power of shewing the connecting links in all human knowledge and inspiring the students to social reorganisation, while the classes on sociology consist of special preparation of young people for practical work on sanitation and kindred subjects, useful enough but representing sociology much as a practical course in chiropody would represent the science of physiology.

Comte wrote two other important essays, one: "Philosophical Considerations on the Sciences and Men of Science", in 1825; the other, "Considerations on the Spiritual Power", in 1826.

But all this time he was preparing his masterpiece the "Positive Philosophy" which was to be the foundation of his life's work.

He held it all in his mind, the work which was to take him twelve years to write, the review of all the abstract scientific knowledge that mankind had attained. Before writing it he decided to give it in seventy-two lectures that he might see what effect it would have on the auditors. He announced these lectures to be held in his house. Men of eminence attended, and when the young Comte saw the audience he was greatly moved and for a moment could not speak. Then, inspired by his subject, he gave the lecture and was listened to with admiring and respectful attention.

Two more of the lectures were given with equal success but when the audience appeared for the fourth there was no lecturer; he was ill, it was said, and the audience retired.

Alas! the moment of his triumph was the moment of his calamity and downfall.

CHAPTER III

POSITIVE CLASSIFICATION

OF THE EIGHTEEN INTERNAL FUNCTIONS OF THE BRAIN

OR SYSTEMATIC VIEW OF THE SOUL

HUMANITY — **PRINCIPAL** — **LIVE FOR OTHERS**

(TO LOVE, TO THINK, TO ACT).
(ACT FROM AFFECTION THINK TO ACT).

- 10 AFFECTIVE MOTORS. Propensities, when active; feelings, when passive.
  - 7 PERSONAL.
    - INTEREST..
      - Instincts of Preservation.......
        - of the individual, or ...... *nutritive instinct*... 1
        - of the race, or *sexual instinct* .. 2; *maternal instinct*... 3
      - Instincts of Improvement.....
        - by destruction or .... *military instinct*... 4
        - by construction, or .... *industrial instinct*... 5
    - AMBITION
      - Temporal, or Pride, desire of power 6
      - Spiritual, or Vanity, desire of approbation 7
    - } Egoism.
  - 3 SOCIAL.
    - Special
      - ATTACHMENT.. 8
      - VENERATION.. 9
    - General
      - BENEVOLENCE, or Universal Love (sympathy) *humanity*.. 10
    - } Altruism.
  - } IMPULSION (THE HEART). Decrease of energy, increase of dignity, from the back of the head to the front, from the lower part to the higher, from the sides to the middle.

MEANS.

- 5 INTELLECTUAL FUNCTIONS.
  - CONCEPTION...
    - Passive or contemplation, hence objective materials
      - Concrete, or relative to Beings, essentially *synthetical*............ 11
      - Abstract, or relative to Events, essentially *analytical* 12
    - Active, or Meditation, hence subjective constructions......
      - Inductive, or by comparison, hence *Generalisation* 13
      - Deductive, or by coordination, hence *Systematisation*....... 14
  - EXPRESSION... Mimic, oral, written, hence *Communication* 15
  - } Knowledge, or vision, for the sake of prevision, with a view to provision.
  - } COUNSEL (THE INTELLECT).

RESULT.

- 3 PRACTICAL QUALITIES.
  - ACTIVITY
    - Courage... 16
    - Prudence... 17
  - FIRMNESS...hence *Perseverance*............................ 18
  - } EXECUTION. (THE CHARACTER).

IN THE JUNGLE

"NEL mezzo del cammin di nostra vita mi retrovai per una silva oscura, che la diritta via era smarrita"—Inf. Canto I.

The moment of his triumph was the moment of his downfall. To realise how this came about his character and surrounding must be clearly understood with the actions and events which led to his sad tragedy. At the head of this chapter is his own "Psycho-analysis" or "Table of the Soul". It is abstract and sums up the desires, intellectual powers, and character of all normal human beings and of the higher animals; the differences of individuals being due to the different proportions of these desires and powers in each case and of the situations in which men are found. All of these desires, personal and social, were strong in Comte, the weakest in proportion was the desire of self-preservation, usually the strongest of all. The instincts of race preservation and of improvement were very marked especially the constructive instinct which has probably never been surpassed in its intensity in any other human being. The desire of approbation was also strong, it was for the approbation of the leading thinkers of his own time and of the future.

All the three social instincts were strong, attachment the least so, to persist with him it seemed to require a mixture of veneration. Veneration was indeed developed to a remarkable degree and, united to his constructive genius, enabled him to gather the past into one harmonious whole, giving to each portion due recognition and honour; it enabled him to avoid the error of the greatest eighteenth century thinkers who in their admiration for classical times so misconceived the middle ages as to call them dark. With regard to the noblest instinct of all, that of benevolence, sympathy, or Humanity, we shall see that his whole life was inspired by his devotion to the future of the race. His mental gifts were of the highest order. Where, indeed, have we seen such powers of observation, generalisation and deduction ? As to the three practical qualities, courage, prudence and perseverance, his courage has already been noticed, his perseverance was almost superhuman as is shown by the work he accomplished in spite of the difficulties by which he was surrounded. In the third practical quality of prudence he was deficient and his ardent feeling and generous impulses, sustained by his fearless courage, led him into actions which caused some of the worst trials of his life.

Like Dante he had to pass through a dark and dismal wood, and like the Red Cross Knight he was not only susceptible to Una, the true love, who leads to Paradise, but also to the wiles of Duessa, the false love, who may drag the soul to the Inferno. When, between thirteen and fourteen years of age, he gave up his belief in the teaching of his mother an ideal feeling for a young woman some years older than himself came to protect him for a short time. She had a kindly affection for him, played to him on the harp, and together they went to listen to beautiful music and had much friendly intercourse. She probably had no idea of the romantic feeling of the boy, but for him this friendship held for the moment all that was beautiful and ennobling, and to the end of his life it remained the first touch of true love. It lasted a very short time, for she married and he was destined to pass thirty years of his life before he was again blessed by that higher feeling. For thirty years he passed under the sway of Duessa; for, unfortunately, soon after this incident he came to the conclusion that he was without beauty or charm, and that no good woman could ever love him. This was in itself a proof of the high ideal he had of women, he did not feel worthy of a true woman's love. Also he passed through the revolutionary stage with great completeness and he tells us later that this was necessary for the work he had to do. He had to put off the old garments before he could put on the new, but the result was a time of moral nudity.

Yet, he was continually finding food for his chivalric feeling. His moral scepticism was only skin deep, beneath it the ascetic and saint were striving to assert themselves, and he was called in his later life " morality intoxicated ". Even at the Lycée the disorder had begun among the boys, as we gather from his letters to Valat, and in Paris the conditions were much worse.

We can hardly form any idea in England of the condition of Paris at that time, for the Catholic religion disappeared much more gradually in England, and later the Puritan movement had much effect, at any rate on opinion and expression. But Paris, where the great hope of the Revolution had been born, and whence the regeneration was to come through this poor boy who went alone to brave its dangers, was at that time the centre of corruption.

Ignorant as she was of so much of the worst evil, his mother Rosalie, vaguely felt the danger.

When he returned to Paris from Montpellier after his expulsion from the Polytechnic his concentration on his work was intense, he was entirely alone, Poinsot found him pupils but does not seem to have given him any social intercourse. No kindly woman noticed, with motherly eye, the young student solitary and uncared for. He had a loving heart and pined for some tenderness but alas, went to seek it among those unhappy girls whose sacrificed lives are the most painful blot on modern civilisation. In his letters to his friend Valat he speaks of these things openly and without remorse or compunction.

It may seem strange that one, who was avowedly working for the regeneration of the human race, should not have felt the incongruity of his action, but it must be remembered that of the three conversions which a modern writer has said every soul must undergo, namely the conversion to truth, to beauty, and to goodness, Auguste had so far only experienced the conversion to truth. True, as a child at his mother's side, he had spontaneously loved goodness and, during his foretaste of love, he had loved beauty, but the full conversion had not come. He was the apostle of truth, all things were to be based on reality, a firm foundation for the religion of the future. This was the task he was called upon to perform, and he was so occupied with the foundation that he did not look up to the superstructure.

Still, he was not satisfied with himself and when he was eighteen he told Valat that he had read the life of Benjamin Franklin and been much impressed by it, it had made him decide to try and give up these undesirable visits and he says he felt better and happier as they might have proved disastrous to him. But he fell back again before long. Indeed, in his latter years he tells us that the fear of personal harm is not a sufficient deterrent from indulgence, a higher motive is necessary.

When he was between nineteen and twenty, he told Valat he had made the acquaintance of a young married lady; she was charming, highly educated, a fine musician, she played to him, taught him Italian, while he gave her some other lesson. He was astonished and very grateful when he found that she loved him. This intercourse was pleasant to him compared with anything that had gone before, but again there is no compunction towards the husband, no mention of him, but many beautiful traits of chivalric feeling are shewn by the young Comte. He speaks of her putting up with privations " with an angelic patience, a charm, a gaiety, a grace, a delicacy of which ordinary women are incapable, but which I also believe examples can only be found in this delightful half of the human race which, taken altogether, is worth infinitely more than the other ".

When a child was born he " accepted the paternity " and then this youth of twenty felt all the wonder of fatherhood and lavished on this little girl the treasure of his affection. His feeling for the mother cooled but he would not forsake " the mother of his child ", and he burst out into a strong expression of how much woman has to bear from man and resolves that as much as possible he will make this up in his own case. This feeling was preparing his heart for the generous but fatal mistake which afterwards so nearly wrecked his life. The child, the little Louise, occupied much of his thought, he was perturbed when she was ill, he did all that was possible under the circumstances to guard and help her, he paid for a sojourn in the country and rejoiced when this had the desired effect on her health.

His companionship with the mother ceased but he never lost sight of the child until her death at nine years of age, and to the end of his life cherished her memory. During this period, in writing to Valat of their friendship, he says:

> " Sweet and tender affections are the happiest, the only source of true well-being that can be attained on this unhappy planet, and it is not possible to have too much of them. Love, fatherhood, far from injuring or being diminished by friendship, unite themselves perfectly with it. These are things which go very well together ".

After this connection was broken off Comte's letters to Valat shew how he longs for friendship and companionship, if only his friend could be near him how happy he would be! and, indeed, it is more than probable that the presence of an intimate and trusted friend would have saved him from the unhappy fate which lay before him. He had sought distraction again as of old, for the strain of his work on his brain must have been very great in his isolation and loneliness, and in May, 1821, he met a young woman who though only nineteen had long lived a life of disorder. She took him home with her and this unhappy acquaintanceship began. Caroline Massin was a beautiful girl, quick and clever, she was the illegitimate daughter of an actress who had handed her over to a young barrister when she was almost a child, he had long abandoned her, and she had fallen so low that her name had been inscribed for two years in a terrible register, by which vice was practically legalised and its unfortunate victims bound to continue their evil life, and to report themselves regularly.

Modern womanhood has arisen and protested against such legal action but apparently there was no help forthcoming for these unfortunate ones at that time in Paris, probably the whole evil was unknown to the more reputable inhabitants as it certainly was to the tender Rosalie in the comparatively simple and innocent surroundings of Montpellier.

Comte was struck by the beauty and intelligence of this girl and they met often. She quickly perceived his simple generosity and from the first suggested marriage, affecting to joke about it, but in the November of that year the barrister who had abandoned her returned and she disappeared. Unfortunately, a year later, Comte met her again. Her intelligence was great and Comte gave her lessons in algebra and she induced him to let them live together. He felt that this would be a steadier life for him and he consented making it, however, quite clear it was only a temporary arrangement. She made him happy, entering into his intellectual work with astonishing understanding, but she was constantly returning to the subject of marriage.

The time was approaching when Comte was to give his lectures, he felt the necessity of a more reputable surrounding, he still thought himself incapable of winning the love of a good woman, and his heart was touched by the unfortunate fate which must lie before Caroline if he forsook her; he hesitated, and at that moment when they were in a café, an officer of the police beckoned her out of the room, she had failed to report herself and had laid herself open to punishment. The officer told her the next day that nothing but marriage could take her name off the register.

Knowing her, as later events showed her, it is almost impossible not to suspect that this was a ruse, she knew the heart of Comte, its generosity, and his fearless contempt of convention. Be that as it may, he could resist no longer, he could not send the woman who had been his bright intelligent companion back to a life of infamy. He consented to the marriage, and having consented carried it out with his usual ardour asking for his parents' consent, a necessity in France. They refused it, for, although they knew nothing of Caroline's career, they heard that she had lived with their son some months before marriage. The unwisdom of the marriage altogether affected the father—a penniless girl, with nothing to recommend her, to a penniless man! but, to Rosalie, the thought that the wife of her beloved son would be impure was indeed terrible. He thought their opposition narrow and heartless and would have obtained an order, which made their consent compulsory, but when they realised that it was useless they withdrew their opposition.

The marriage took place, the officer of police attended and took the name off the register, and, that the past might be unknown, one of the witnesses was the barrister Circlet connected with Caroline's past. One solemn promise Comte exacted from Caroline, it was that she should never again have any communication with Circlet by interview or letter. This promise she gave.

Comte thought he had secured a companion who would be bound to him always by gratitude. It has been contended that he loved her, but he himself tells us that he committed this chief error of his life without love, and we need no other evidence of this than his looking for gratitude, for love knows itself the debtor and does not seek, but feels gratitude.

His hope was soon dimmed, he took his wife to Montpellier to introduce her to his parents and friends who were astonished at her beauty, intelligence and fine manners. She was a Parisienne with all the " savoir faire " of a Parisienne. Had love or gratitude had any place in her heart she would have been delighted to meet her husband's people and to win the love of his mother, but she found the simple life of Montpellier intolerably dull. They only stayed a fortnight and Comte returned, perturbed and anxious. On which side did the fault lie ?

He evidently felt pretty sure. The ready wit and good manners which had been admired at Montpellier were a poor foundation for a peaceful domestic life. He had dreamed that they should go to live at Montpellier and be surrounded by friends, and he would once again be near those he loved. For necessary as Paris had been at the beginning of his career, and for the preparation of his work, it was so no longer. The work was all prepared in his brain and needed only a quiet harmonious surrounding to enable him to put it before the world in the shortest possible time.

He realised however that they must live in Paris where his wife would be. The one thing that mattered was the completion of his task, and to this he turned with his accustomed energy. It had to be continued without the peaceful surrounding he had hoped to secure by his marriage. His domestic life was a stormy one. Madame Comte was not only without the feeling of contented gratitude he had expected to find in her, but, having gained her point, she felt contempt for that which she considered his weakness ; she begun to think she could rule him completely. Quick and astute as she was to see the intellectual powers which would enable him to win for her a distinguished position in the world, it was impossible for her to understand the greatness of his heart or his intense determination. His marriage had been the result of the thoroughness with which he carried out his opinions to their logical conclusions.

Senhor Mendes, one of his most devoted followers, has well pointed out that in times of anarchy it is the noble souls who suffer most from the disorder, just because they are less under the control of custom and are prepared to do what others only profess. How many a less noble and generous soul must have been faced with the same problem as Auguste Comte but did not try to save and protect his comrade !

Remembering her upbringing, Comte bore with his wife and tried to excuse her but she was not only lacking in purity and faithfulness she also seems to have been devoid of tenderness or delicacy of feeling. Slowly the realisation of this dawned on Comte. However, she was often a pleasant, intelligent, and helpful companion, and he had married with the full intention of attaching himself completely to her. During that first year his times of misery were frequent and heart-rending. He began to feel that the only refuge for him was indifference, and that he dreaded; indeed, to one of his temperament, indifference to the one being with whom he was in intimate connection was impossible. At last, after a year of marriage, she proposed to him that Cerclet should be allowed to visit them regardless of her solemn promise, and on Comte's refusal left his roof for a time.

The shock to him was intense. It was practically a proposal that he, who had striven to save her from a life of dishonour, should share in the price of his own dishonour. The shock came just at the moment when the strain of his work was at its highest, and when the recognition of his claims by some of the most eminent men of his time had produced an exaltation and hope which he had not before experienced. It seemed that the realisation of his highest hopes was at hand and, at this moment, she, to whom he had given the shelter of his home, the friend in whom he trusted, believed that he could pass over the breaking of a solemn promise and offered to him the most degrading position that it is possible for a man to occupy,—and how deeply his heart was wounded. She preferred the man who had left her to misery and shame and forgot him who had placed her at his right hand. What wonder that a paroxysm of rage took possession of him. The course of lectures, which was already bringing him into fame was interrupted and, filled with passion and indignation, he rushed to his friend Lammenais, and threw himself at his feet and, under the seal of confession, told him the story of his marriage and its results, hoping thus to relieve the fearful pressure on his brain. It was not enough, he could not go home again, and later was found at Montmorency where Madame, *accompanied by Cerclet*, and summoning Blainville the eminent physician to her aid, went to find him. That she should have taken Cerclet with her shows an almost incredible coarseness and lack of feeling.

Blainville found him in a state of over mental excitement, bordering on alienation, but mania at that time had not set in. He advised Madame Comte to take him home and give him complete rest and quiet, he told her that to take him to an asylum would probably excite him and make him worse. She refused unless Blainville would undertake to stay with her. He could not do this and so Comte was taken to the private asylum of M. Esquirol. They told him he was to be taken home and there is every indication that he might even then have been saved, for his wife had come for him; perhaps she loved and cared for him after all! It seems he did not see Cerclet. He laid his head on her shoulder, then on her knees, affection was still there for him. He was to be taken home, he hoped to sleep, the soothing quiet was descending on the overworn brain when he suddenly realised that they were not taking him home, that he was to be put in confinement, separated from his work, from his home, and from the wife whose returning care and affection he had hoped for. He was seized with an access of fury which, after he had been incarcerated, resulted in mania.

Madame Comte, in writing to Montpellier, simply said he was not well and was staying in the country, but her father, to whom she had refused money, wrote to Comte's parents telling them where he was and of the conduct of his wife and her former history. This was indeed a blow for the simple family at

Montpellier, whose hopes for their brilliant son were dashed to the ground. His mother decided to go to him, and arranged with the father that she should bring him back and in the quiet and peace of their surroundings strive to calm and restore the troubled brain.

She started at once, and on her arrival in Paris went straight to the Asylum and saw her son. He did not recognise her but, from his words and the information she had, she perceived the cause of his alienation, and formed her opinion about the case. She felt that the treatment and constraint were aggravating the disease and asked to be allowed to take her son with her, but Esquirol refused, saying, he could only hand him over to his wife who had entrusted him to his care.

The devoted mother then put aside her prejudice and sought her daughter-in-law and proposed to her that they should take him out and place him in a religious house to be cured there. This his wife refused and in this she was probably right, for Rosalie, the pious mother, imagined that the soothing influence of the religion would gradually calm his mind and even bring him back to his old simple faith, but his wife knew this to be impossible, and perhaps felt that such a surrounding would only irritate him further.

Esquirol had promised a speedy cure, so the mother waited in Paris, but the cure did not come and, after a few months, Esquirol pronounced the case incurable. Here Comte would have been left, his work lost to the world, but the mother with the wonderful insight of love, thought differently, she believed that if all the causes of irritation were removed he would recover. She sought her daughter-in-law again asking her whether she would take him back to his old home and tend him there promising all the pecuniary help she could give by the utmost economy of her own concerns. To this his wife consented and he was brought home with an attendant, the windows being barred by the advice of Esquirol.

To the mind of Rosalie, with her earnest Catholic convictions, their marriage had been no real marriage, it had not been blessed by the Church, what but further evil could result from their living together under such conditions? So, before she left them, by the aid of Lammenais, the nuptial benediction was pronounced, Comte all unconscious of the ceremony which would have seemed to him a mockery. Then the mother clasped her son in her arms and, as she had dedicated him as an infant, so now she offered herself as an oblation in his place, with intense religious devotion, and then returned home. Her son did not know that she had been there and she never told him of her devotion, thus helping towards his cure, for he thought it had all been the doing of his wife and the intense irritation her infidelity had caused him was soothed by her apparent fidelity and attachment.

Soon it was found necessary to remove the bars and dismiss the attendant, these things irritated the patient, then the calm, the quiet, the feeling that he was cared for, gradually cured him, and the excitement passed away from the brain. But the reaction was inevitable, he was not allowed to work, his private life offered him little hope for the future, and profound depression set in. What use was he? What good was his life to himself or others! The thought became intolerable and one day he went out and threw himself from the top of the Pont des Arts into the Seine. A member of the Royal Guard, crossing the bridge, saw a drowning man and jumped in to his rescue; little thinking, and probably never knowing, what important service he was rendering to the world.

The shock had completed the work of cure and as he recovered he not only regretted the anxiety he had caused his wife, but the feeling of his mission returned, and he felt he had been guilty of an act of cowardice in trying to escape his suffering. He waited for returning strength, preparing himself to resume his work when possible. He also formed the resolution to endure patiently in his domestic life. Caroline was his wife, and must live with him, and he must not ask for tenderness, accepting what she gave him he would not allow her action to interfere with the task it was given him to accomplish.

The pecuniary difficulty was great but Ternau, a rich industrialist, responded to his request for help and, after a time, he was able to resume his lessons to earn his dailybread and then to take up again the work which had been so sadly interrupted.

CHAPTER IV

THE FOUNDATION

COMTE had to take up his life's work very gradually. The necessity for precautions as to health and strain, which he had never taken before, became evident. The struggle for daily bread, it was a hard one, had to be maintained, but his resolution was indomitable and his thoughts were occupied with the work to be done.

His first important writing after his recovery, an essay on Broussais' "Cerebral Irritation and Madness", throws much light on his strength of mind. With calm philosophic insight he used his own experience, during his residence in the asylum, both as to symptoms and treatment, throwing much light on the subject and making the essay of special value.

After this, he returned to the lectures so abruptly broken off and gave the whole series in the year. The same eminent men gathered to hear them, shewing their confidence in his complete cure. They listened, enthralled, to the clear exposition of the young philosopher as in the course of seventy-two lectures he expounded the history and philosophy of the abstract sciences, mathematics, astronomy, physics, chemistry, biology, and sociology, and it must be remembered that among those who listened admiringly were specialists in each branch. Poinsot and Navier, the eminent mathematicians, Humbolt, the astronomer, whose world-wide fame endures, Fourier, the physicist, whose researches on heat were translated sixty years later for the Cambridge University Press, Blainville, the biologist and physician, whose scale of animals was the best then compiled, and Broussais, the follower of Bichat, to whose work, with that of his master, the development of positive science in connection with medicine is largely due.

The situation is unique in the history of the race. Comte had, in his brain, before his illness, and found there unimpaired on his recovery, the whole of his positive philosophy which afterwards occupied six volumes. It is true he amplified it a little in parts but in essentials it was the same. It was, indeed, a miracle of intellectual achievement and he who gave it was himself founder of sociology, the summit of the series. It is impossible in a short life of this kind to give a complete idea of the scope and value of this work which is little known in England, our universities having ignored it in their courses. Comte, in later years, thought it unnecessary that it should be read except by those learned men who should respond to his call and form themselves into the new spiritual society to unite Europe and reorganise the world.

A few principal points in the work and in his mind at the time it is necessary to recall that we may follow his later development. In his early days his interest was concentrated on two subjects, his belief in science and his desire for social regeneration. The discovery of the sociological laws, when he was twenty-four, united these two aims, for, by carrying law into political and social questions, the regeneration was securely founded on science. Knowing himself scientifically prepared he hoped to construct the renovating doctrine at once and wrote his essay on the Spiritual Power. But he soon saw that the foundation of scientific doctrine must also be given to the world, that social philosophy must be shewn to rest on natural philosophy, or the life of man to depend on the laws of the world. It was then that eighty hours of thought resulted in the conception of the Positive Philosophy as the foundation of the regeneration.

Two special tasks lay before him, one mental, the other social. In the one, sociology would be shewn as the summit of scientific observations from the Greek times to Comte's own day. Here, the method was necessarily objective passing from the world to man, and the process of extracting the positive part of each science from the mass of theological and metaphysical ideas still surrounding it implied discussion. In the later work, the subjective would be the necessary point of view, passing from man to the world, and the treatment would be more dogmatic.

The object of the philosophy was to establish social physics as celestial, terrestial and organic physics had been established. This would give the positive view universality and would, therefore, lead to mental harmony, this harmony being impossible while some ideas are explained by theology or metaphysics and some by positivism. But the most ardent theologian does not claim that we should return to theology in all the affairs of life, therefore the only harmony lies in bringing all under the shelter of the positive spirit. All the lower sciences are of importance to men but unity has been lost sight of in specialisation, the divisions between the sciences are arbitrary and for convenience, in reality they are one. We cannot go back but must go forward and create a class of specialists in generalisation (this is the Spiritual Power). The first result of the philosophy will be to give us guidance in our search for truth, the second, the recasting of education. What is needed is that the methods and general conception of the abstract sciences shall be taught in a manner comprehended by the mass of the people.

The sciences are classified according to their decreasing generality and increasing dependence, and are related to space, earth and Humanity. Mathematics, the foundation of all, can only be proved on the mental space, that is to say in the mind.

Scientific men and others in England and Italy have declared Comte's work to be antiquated because new discoveries have been made since his time. The French do not seem to have made the same mistake, probably because they are more accustomed to distinguish the abstract from the concrete. His work was abstract and he does not claim to be a scientist, except in sociology, though he well might have done so in mathematics, and it was said of him by an eminent man of his own day that " no science held any secret for him ".

He meets this objection himself when he says of the special class of thinkers that their work will throw light on the work of the specialists, and adds, " *whose results the specialists would in turn be able to rectify* ". Far from limiting the development of the mind, his discovery of " Relativity " shews that truth is nothing fixed but a quantity varying with every age, nay, with every day, of the life of Humanity. He certainly classified and arranged human knowledge so that any new material can be at once utilised. As well might a librarian be accused of not wanting any more books in his library because he has arranged those he has; is it not rather true that until he has arranged them the most valuable new books will be practically useless to the public?

He traced the whole growth of mathematics from the early Greek discoveries up to the modern analytic method re-defining geometry as the *indirect* measurement of magnitudes and substituting " volume " for " solid ", as, in the mental space, we imagine the impression or shape rather than the solid itself. He showed how number underlies all human conceptions and how the abstract laws of motion of Kepler, Newton, and Galileo may be traced even in social phenomena. The sciences are divided into inorganic and organic and the inorganic again into the celestial and terrestrial. The abstract astronomy of the solar system is really mathematics made manifest; this science has cleared itself of theology and metaphysics. Physics, combined with chemistry, is the study of the earth; the branches of physics correspond with our senses by aid of which our observations are made. Physics consists in the study of the general laws of matter while chemistry deals with the special. In physics man begins to modify the world and thus helps to overcome the theological spirit as astronomy does by the clear prevision it admits. Here experiment is developed while in chemistry clear and accurate definition aids the mind. The problem of chemistry is: from the compound to find the elements, or vice versa; its phenomena approach very near to those of life.

In biology the composition and decomposition (found in chemistry) takes place round a centre. Life is defined by Blainville as "the double interior action of composition and decomposition". For this, an organism and a sympathetic environment are necessary. The study of biology is divided into that of vegetable and animal, and the vegetable, as simpler, is the foundation of the more complex animal life. Comparison is the method developed and in the scale we descend from man to the vegetable or ascend from the vegetable to man. The problem is: "given the organ to find the function, and vice versa".

The animal life serves the vegetable, that is, it enables the being to find food, or its mate, and to avoid danger. Only when man living in society has brought into being an immense and practically eternal life is this reversed, and the vegetable life then serves the animal or the life of nutrition the life of relation. Each science rests on all below it and in education the same order of gradual complication should be followed.

The introductory chapters to all the sciences have been slightly indicated here. In each case Comte proceeded to deal with the whole history and growth of the science and he did it as we have seen to the satisfaction and admiration of the most eminent specialists of the day. He then expounded the science of sociology of which he is the acknowledged founder. So far his work had been to arrange the work of others disentangling the positive thought, founded on observation and reality, from the theologic and metaphysic thought founded on fiction and imagination. Now, his work was creative.

The theologic solution has failed before the positive is established and revolution is the result, men are divided into camps of so-called Order or Progress, the one clinging to the past order without appreciating its development, the other largely negative calling vaguely for progress, and men oscillate between the two as they are alarmed, (as in the foolish panic in our day in England over the Zinovief letter). But order and progress are not opposed, no government can last unless based on order, or if it be opposed to progress.

The positive principle recognises the law of

continuous human development, its aim is the establishment of mental harmony on the basis of order and it is directly progressive, it does not seek absolute truth but is always relative and makes prevision possible in social matters as in physical. The science is divided into static and dynamic investigations, that is, the conditions of society and the laws of its development. All the means of investigation employed in the simpler sciences are utilised in sociology with the addition of historic observation. It rests on all the other sciences. There are three aspects in which man can be regarded: (1) Individual, (2) Family, (3) Society. In the first, we see feeling is stronger than intellect and the personal desires are stronger than the social; the problem is to modify these selfish desires by the union of social feeling and intellectual activity. In the second, the family is the unit of society, containing all its elements and through it man comes forth from personality and learns to live for others. Man and woman in the family correspond to the Temporal and Spiritual Powers in society. In the third, Society, we find unity of aim with diversity of means, co-operation prevails. There can be no society without government and this consists of two parts, Temporal and Spiritual, at first combined then separate. The spirit of the whole must prevail and combine the parts.

The "Law of the Three Stages" is the basis of social dynmics, by its aid Comte traced the growth of society with marvellous power and insight from the times of primitive savagery up to his own day, passing in review the fetichist, astrolatric, polytheist, monotheist, and revolutionary periods.

It is very difficult for us to-day to realise the immensity of this labour or the originality of thought it implied. For, although he himself has been little recognised, his thought has permeated society so that every superficial history and schoolboy's primer has caught the idea of continuous development, the realisation of the full mental harmony is, however, still far off. In summing up, Comte says: "Positive philosophy confines research to the invariable relations which constitute natural laws." We cannot limit the extension of man's knowledge but it must advance by the path of observation and experience, it is in accordance with common sense.

Science has been prized as the basis of rational action but its logical effect in developing the mind is also of importance and the firm mental foundation allows liberty of conception and speculation. The establishment of positivism will modify society far more than any revolution yet experienced. In speculation men will be spared much labour by the rational method, the concentration of man's hopes on the earth will stimulate all speculations which will improve the conditions of existence. Moral rules will acquire energy and tenacity when men realise how the actions and feelings of each affect the lives of others, a common belief will give effect to conviction and a universal education will unite all. Personal morality will be ennobled when it is detached from ideas of prudence with regard to physical health or eternal salvation. The importance of domestic life will be realised as it is there that the virtues are learned and the sweetness of living for others made manifest, and, in social life positive morality will show that our happiness depends on the habit of benevolent acts and sympathetic feelings. Relativity will make it applicable to all cases. In politics the separation of the powers of command and counsel will secure order and progress. Every form of noble art will find expression beyond anything known in the past as the conquest of man over nature is recognised and all the surroundings of man brought into sympathetic relations with him.

The "Philosophy" was finished in 1842 when Comte was forty-four years old. The foundation of his life's work was laid. He had created the science of sociology but had not yet perceived the higher step of disentangling the science of the individual in society from that of the animal man in biology, and from that of society itself. He had shown that the problem was the subordination of personal to social feeling, that the aim was love, but he had not yet realised that the motive power was also love, which thus becomes the Alpha and Omega of Humanity.

CHAPTER V

The Path Through the Desert

HOW was Comte upheld by his family and friends during the twelve years of concentrated labour which resulted in the completion of his "Philosophy", the foundation of his life's work, his social mission?

The story of his gradually increasing isolation and suffering is indeed a sad one and is intimately connected with his unhappy marriage. The chivalry of his nature made him uphold the woman he had married against all the world and after his recovery he decided to put her past infidelity entirely out of his mind for he felt now he owed her a debt of gratitude, not only had she nursed him back to life but he thought she had also saved him for his work. He had heard that his mother had been induced by Lammenais to try to place him in a religious house and he believed this was a plot of the Catholic Church to keep him incarcerated, and prevent the carrying out of his mission. This distrust of his friend Lammenais was increased when he found his wife's history was known, and believed that Lammenais had betrayed what he had told him under the seal of confession. He did not know that Caroline's father had been spreading reports about her and that there were many other channels through which the knowledge of her past might have been spread. It turned him for a time against Lammenais and had the unfortunate effect of making him doubt whether his mother's religion might not induce her to turn against him. His wife could have told him of his mother's devotion during his illness, but it is evident she did not, and this helped to bring about his separation from his family which can only be regarded with deep regret.

He insisted on respect being shown to his wife and would not have anyone in his house who treated her with disrespect. Tabarié whose friendship had been highly valued by Comte and who had helped with money during his illness wrote after his recovery saying his marriage had been a fatal mistake. Comte immediately broke off all correspondence with him and this helpful friendship passed out of his life, though never out of his heart. His illness also caused a break in his correspondence with Valat, and for some years there was silence between these two devoted friends. His friend Eichthall joined the St. Simonians and entirely changed his attitude of respectful friendship towards the man who had taught him so much.

His sister, Alix, had spoken strongly against his wife even telling her parents that if she came to Montpellier she herself would go into a convent during her visit. How this was reported in Paris we do not know but there seem to have been some gossips in Montpellier. Alix also had some controversy with Auguste on theological matters. His mother's letters became more and more pathetic, she implored him to write oftener and to write to his sister who was ill, she sent kind messages to his wife, but finally, during an outbreak of cholera in Paris, she asked him to come alone to Montpellier. Then his anger broke out. Should he seek safety himself and leave the being who was the most to him in the world in danger! His letter was very bitter; Caroline should be respected as his wife. He would never go alone, he would write no more.

He might have recognised as part of the situation that there could be no real sympathy between the simple orthodox family at Montpellier and the brilliant, emancipated, pleasure-loving Caroline, but his gradually increasing misery at home was making him irritable and bitter, he would, if possible, hide the fact that his hearth fire was dead. Outside criticism of his wife touched him on the raw, he was realising more and more that he had ruined the peace and happiness of his life by his loveless quixotic marriage.

After his recovery from his illness he had reconsidered his life and regulated it anew. It had always been a life of sustained endeavour with little self-indulgence but now he felt he must guard his health if he were to perform his life's task. He would no longer keep himself awake night after night that he might continue his meditation, he had done so by drinking coffee and this he now gave up entirely, and in later days he made other renunciations to mark crises in his life.

He gave seven or eight hours to sleep, six or eight were taken up every day by the lessons which supplied him and his wife with their daily bread, he took long solitary walks to avoid undue strain on the brain, and, if we deduct the necessary time for meals and some slight social intercourse, we find he had little time left for the beloved task which was the purpose of his life. Even that short time was diminished by the want of harmony with his wife, by their differences of opinion and outlook.

She dared once more, just at the end of his course of lectures in 1829, to repeat the infamous proposal she had made before that she should receive a rich gallant. This time, while rejecting it with horror, Comte did not allow it to upset his health. He had begun to accept her at her own valuation and not to expect fidelity or purity from her. She was constantly urging him to seek for appointments and once induced him to take political action, but the authorities were against him, and in politics he found that those he was working with believed in a very different republicanism to his own. They wanted to bring about changes immediately and by violence, while his method was by conviction and rational understanding.

A characteristic incident took place in 1830 when the political situation was grave. Summoned to join the National Guard, Comte, refusing to do so, was condemned by the Council of Discipline, but defended himself and, giving his reasons for being a conscientious objector, said,—

> "The law declares that the National Guard is founded to defend the Government which France has chosen. Had it been only to maintain order I should not have refused my part in the duties this law imposed, but I refuse to take part in purely political struggles. I shall never attack the Government by force, but being republican in heart and mind I cannot take the oath to defend at the peril of my life and of that of others a government which I should oppose were I a man of action".

He was condemned to three days in prison. He prepared at once to go providing himself with a large quantity of paper, ink, sealing wax, and, it is said, thirty books, while he arranged with his pupils to come to the prison for their lessons. He went off and Madame Comte, left behind, felt anxious for she knew how any change in his arrangements upset him. There was a ring at the door, it was the good natured Guard who had brought her a pass to save her the trouble of going for it. He said he would much rather carry out his orders against people who resisted than against one who carried them out himself so pleasantly. It is also said that Comte was rather sorry when his three days' retirement came to an end.

In 1832, he was appointed as Tutor in the Polytechnic and, in 1837 was made Examiner, and these posts gave him more time for his work. He bore with his wife as he best could but sometimes his chivalry failed him and he taxed her with ingratitude to the man who had given her his name. She disdainfully rejected the idea that she owed him gratitude, indeed it is evident that such a woman, ambitious, pleasure-seeking, capable, conscious of being able to shine in society, must have found little to suit her in the lonely and penurious life she led by the side of this man so austerely devoted to his work. She must have felt like a lover of money who held a cheque for a large amount which no one would cash, for she knew her husband's power and genius and realised all that he might have done and been, and he would do nothing to lead to the life of ease and distinction of which she dreamed. He gave way to her in so many ways that she thought him weak and did not understand that it was the strength of his determination to put up with the evils resulting from his choice. She left him more than once that she might be free. At first he begged her to return but the day came when he told her that if she went again it must be never to return. She did not believe he would carry this threat into effect and left him in 1842 never again to enter his house until he lay dead within it.

His long misery came to an end but he had not escaped scathless; how was it possible that he should! He had entirely respected her as his wife and never, in spite of her long absences, was unfaithful to her. But no man was ever more susceptible to woman's influence, and hers had a hardening effect upon him, there are signs of a certain drying up of his heart, he was severe with those who opposed him and his opinion about women was lowered, he did not expect from them a higher standard of personal morality than that among men.

Had Comte's work been merely intellectual research for its own sake, this drying up of the heart would have been fatal, but the social purpose of his work was never absent from his mind. The love of the children of the future was burning in his heart, and was his salvation. But his own life was marred, his nature " cribbed, cabined and confined ".

We are constantly told to-day of the evil effect on development of too great repression of the lower instincts but how disastrous when the higher ones have little or no sustenance, when the tender attachment and loving veneration which should take root and flourish in family life are left to wither there unfostered. These should have sustained him in his abnormal development of the highest instinct of all, his devotion to the future. The strain of that devotion without their aid must have been great and caused the bitterness, the harsh judgment, with which he has been taxed.

When in his studies he arrived at the sociology which was exclusively his own domain, he was necessarily led to study the arts and here, at last, his nature found expansion. In the works of the most renowned poets of all the Western countries he found the help which he needed for his higher, nobler feeling. He deeply regretted that music, poetry, and painting had been denied him in his early days and, later, when he came to deal with the education of the young, he stressed the importance of these things. His life so far had been absorbed in keen intellectual endeavour. It was not enough; he was beginning to realise the importance of beauty.

In 1837 his mother, Rosalie, died. Directly he heard she was ill he wrote but his letter was too late, she was never conscious enough to hear that it had come. There is no record of that letter but we can guess that it bore the message of the tender love for her which had lain dormant in his heart. What bitter grief and self-upbraiding he felt we cannot know but his later words and reviving worship of her can give us some idea. Her death, his domestic sorrows, and other difficulties, caused a short breakdown in his health and on recovery he made another personal renunciation, that of tobacco.

For a few more years his wife lived with him and then she left him as we have seen, and so, through no act of his, he was left alone. What he endured in their life together we can guess when we hear that loneliness and complete isolation were peaceful and happy to him by comparison.

CHAPTER VI

The Meeting

HIS wife had left him but her sinister effect on his life was not ended, even after he had found rest in death his work was retarded both in France and England by the misunderstanding of his relationship with her. For the moment he lived in comparative peace; he speaks of it as " the peace of the grave ".

He was alone in the large apartment of the Rue Monsieur le Prince where he and his wife had moved some time before their separation, where the strenuous work of his later years was done, where he experienced the regeneration of his heart and mind by means of a noble affection, where he died attended by his adopted daughter and faithful disciples; and where to-day, seventy years after his death, men from all lands come to meditate on the life and work of the wise and loving social Reformer and religious Teacher.

The work which had occupied every moment he could spare from bread winning was finished and the relief from strain was great. He lived more and more with the poets and listened to beautiful music, the esthetic side of his nature developed apace. But more was needed, his bitter experience had hardened him and made him harsh. He wrote a preface to the last volume of his "Positive Philosophy" in which he attacked Arago a leading member of the French Academy, and the whole system of which he formed part. He pointed out how unjustly he had been treated when he had applied for posts in the Polytechnic; this was indeed true, for, in spite of his extraordinary ability for mathematical teaching and his reputation for the philosophy of science, he had been passed over again and again for less able men.

The severe attack on Arago alarmed Comte's publisher who showed the preface to Arago and altered it. Comte brought an action against him for doing this, claiming the freedom of the press. The cause was given in his favour but the incident created a feeling of bitter hostility against him in the Academy which led later to his monetary ruin and the loss of his posts at the Polytechnic, although he left an impression there of a high and honourable character and of undoubted mental superiority. As examiner he raised the whole standard of the school. He was honoured alike by his pupils, his fellow-teachers and his official superiors but he found the lack of intellectual honesty and mental capacity in high places was unendurable and when he spoke against it his words had no uncertain sound. His post as examiner gave him his first opportunity of travel, he saw many of the towns of France and had pleasant contacts with many people. He soon wearied of the enforced absence, Paris was the scene of his life's work and there he would be. But during his time of misery at home the change must have been a relief and it benefitted his health and also enabled him to renew his relations with his early friend Valat. Valat, however, could not comprehend his work and made some inadequate criticisms of the philosophy, and later confessed that he had returned to Catholicism. Although surprised at this change Comte congratulated him at having at any rate returned to the logical theology and not stopped at any of the half-way deistic houses. His pleasant expansions to Valat about his work were necessarily over and the loneliness of his heart is expressed when he says that he loves his friend's children but feels how much he has lost by having none of his own. He loved animals too, observed them closely and recognised their devotion. In a letter to his wife on one of his examining tours he speaks of "notre pauvre Toulon" who was a little cat that had been given them. His visits to Montpellier as examiner were embittered by the fact that his father and sister did not see him. Even at this time he was not entirely forsaken; a year before she left him Madame Comte had engaged a household help, Sophie Bliaux (Madame Thomas) who looked after his bodily needs with pious care. Comte did not at first realise what she was, for this humble woman was to become one of the "three Queens who helped him in his need" and was to earn the gratitude of all who loved and honoured him.

Through the cloud which hung over his life there

shines the constant light of his social ardour, his whole heart was set on doing the work for which his previous labours were but a preparation, his love of the race never failed but no man can live on this highest spiritual bread alone; he was like a man climbing a mountain whose provisions which were to help him on the way had failed. Some personal appreciation fell to his share and of this he made the most.

His work was recognised by eminent men in Europe, notably by Littré, in France, who spoke of himself as a little•boy by his side, and by John Stuart Mill, in England, who acknowledged him as his master. With him he formed a friendship through correspondence and Mill's letters shew the admiration he felt for the French philosopher. He was not able to follow him in his later work but at this time they were in accord and Mill quoted Voltaire's saying that when a Frenchman and an Englishman agree they must be right. Comte remarked that, while the mass of the English people were very much behind those on the continent, their few thinkers were more advanced, and certainly the work of Bacon, Locke, Hume and others confirms this testimony. Mill, in an early letter, apologised to Comte for the concessions he had to make to Anglican opinion. He says that a writer speaking out would not only lose his social position (which he would be prepared to do) but would also not be read, he himself simply refrained from the declamatory praises of providential wisdom which were generally made use of even by unbelievers in

England. It is to be hoped our writers of to-day have the courage of their opinions whatever they may be.

He made the acquaintance of the Austins who were in Paris and his friendship with Mrs. Austin, though slight, was a real pleasure to him. So far the women of intellectual eminence he had known were either blue stockings, that is, suffering from pride of intellect, or " femmes libres ", having cast aside the current morality; in her, he found both " intellectual modesty and moral delicacy ". She accused him in a letter of not sufficiently appreciating women. He was much disturbed by this accusation and told her that while he expected only about fifty people in the whole of Europe to understand his work and give him their adhesion he had always thought a large proportion of them would be women, adding, he should distrust any system that did not appeal to them. On a fuller knowledge of his work, Mrs. Austin wrote to him that on the woman question " there is only you ", " Il n'y a que vous ". Writing to her on the subject of prayer, he says:

> " Prayer has its indestructible basis in human nature. People think that the emotions and even the conceptions of our nature cannot exist apart from the costume they wore during childhood ".

In 1843, he wrote his treatise on Analytic Geometry and, in 1844, his " Popular Astronomy ". Ever since 1830 he had given a free course of lectures on astronomy to workmen. He felt the importance of their realising the scientific method that they might apply it, rather than the merely critical or destructive method, to social questions. Through all his difficulties he continued these seventy lectures a year until 1847. They were much appreciated by the Parisian workmen and an increasing number attended, of all sorts and conditions, reaching, one year, a total of four hundred. Some of his most devoted followers both in life and after death were drawn from this source. Although the lectures lasted two, three or even, in some cases, for five hours, with a short interval in the middle, it was rare indeed for any of the hearers to leave before the end. His style, a little formal at the beginning of the lecture, recalling his writings, became animated, charming and conversational as he developed his subject; never losing the central theme or thread of the discourse he illustrated it with astonishing vividness using swift sarcasm, and pleasant irony to emphasise the points he wished to make, while his own intense belief carried conviction to the audience. His voice was clear and without being loud was heard in every corner of the room. It is said that those who were present at these lectures could never forget them.

In 1844 the hatred of the Academy began to have its effect. The examinership for the Polytechnic was taken from him, and this meant that the sale of his " Analytic Geometry " ceased. The loss of the post in a preparatory school followed, and Comte was reduced to his position as lecturer. He tried to get lessons in the schools but the principals were either convinced by, or feared to offend, the opinion of the Academy. His own needs were very modest, his life was even ascetic, but he had undertaken to pay Madame Comte three thousand francs a year and this was a large share of his slender resources.

The members of the Academy hoped to silence him but he was already known in Europe, and it is to the credit of England that the first to come to his assistance were three Englishmen whom Mill had informed of his difficulties. Grote, Molesworth and Raikes Currie sent him a sufficient sum expressing their indignation at the treatment he had received from the Polytechnic.

About this time one of Comte's pupils, Maximilien Marie, wrote a treatise on mathematics of which the Academy took no notice. Comte regarded the work favourably and to the next edition Marie added a dedication to him in which he expressed his respect for the master. He lived with his parents and no doubt he spoke of Comte in his family. At the end of 1844 Maximilien Marie invited him to his home, he introduced him to his fair young wife, little more than a child, and then, turning to another lady who was in the room, he introduced his sister. As she rose to greet him Comte bowed and then raised his shortsighted eyes (one was weak and drooping) and saw before him a young woman rather above the middle height, of graceful and modest bearing, with fair auburn hair making an aureole around her head, with a bright and beautiful colour in her cheeks, soft green eyes and an expression which showed how prolonged suffering had given a pensive caste to features naturally formed for gladness and joy. Auguste Comte looked for the first time on the face of Clotilde de Vaux. He was visibly struck, here was the gentle goodness, the feminine charm, which he had so far sought in vain, perhaps death who had even then laid his hand upon her had already given her the transformation which is his special gift, and the spiritual had already conquered the physical.

As he took his leave Clothilde turned to her young sister-in-law and said with something of her old girlish gaiety " How ugly he is ".

CHAPTER VII

"Ella Che Imparadisa La Mia Mente"

CLOTILDE DE VAUX, the sister of Maximilien Marie and the daughter of Captain and Madame Marie, united in herself the two opposite strains then so marked in France; on her mother's side she was descended from the old French aristocracy, and it was among them, when they were not corrupted, that the finest development of personal grace and refinement of the Western world was found; and on her father's side she came from the people, that French proletariat full of the passionate social impulse which was the moving power in the regeneration of the modern world. Her mother's family, the de Ficquelmonts, were not only aristocrats but also had shewn remarkable intellectual powers. Their hereditary property was in Lorraine and they were one of the four families called "Les Grands Chevaux" who formed the four pillars of the ducal throne. They were related to the first houses of Europe and boasted cousinship to the holy and illustrious Archbishop of Milan, Saint Charles Borroméo, they claimed also relationship to a very different character the Comte de la Marche, the " Wild Boar of the Ardennes " of whom Sir Walter Scott has written in " Quentin Durward ".

Clotilde's uncle, the Count de Ficquelmont, was of a noble character and once controlled a large mob, collected to assassinate his cousin, by his calmness and dauntless bearing. In the latter part of his life he devoted himself to literature. In a book called " Lord Palmerston, England and the Continent ", he analysed the situation of European societies and shewed the certain ruin of the ancient order, the difficulties of the new organisation, and the impossibility of returning to the past. The chivalry of his character is shewn in a letter he wrote to his daughter, on the day of her confirmation, in which he pointed out that the moral life is a constant struggle, and urged her to use the gifts and advantages she had received with gratitude, and to remember that " all men were equal before God ", and he described to her the life of a woman and how it differs from that of a man.

The sister of this Count was Henriette Josephine Marie, the mother of Clotilde, she also was mentally well endowed and liberal in mind. She wrote many pamphlets on social economy full of the love of humanity, one was a " Suggestion for a religious and perpetual association of women to work for the help of the poor and the extirpation of mendicity ". Her liberal opinions probably led to her marriage with Captain Marie, a man of the people, whom she met in Bohemia when she was thirty-six. For this marriage she was for a time thrown off by her family.

Clotilde was born in Paris on the 2nd of April, 1815. Captain Marie had retired from the army and he and his wife were poor but through her interest he was appointed collector of taxes at Meru in 1823. Clotilde's parents can have had little devotion to the Catholic Church for she was not baptised until she was nine years old, and then, apparently, only as a means of admission to the Convent of the Legion of Honour, where she was admitted as a pupil and remained until she was eighteen. Here she became a devout Catholic.

Louis XVIII had established order with toleration, and catholics of large outlook had brought about a partial re-birth of catholicism which inspired the young and penetrated to the convent school where the child Clotilde was being educated giving her the training in reverence which helped to make her the woman she became. This discipline developed in noble minds the tendency to self-sacrifice, to voluntary submission, and to constant self-examination lest self should prevail, and Clotilde, whose soul was attuned to all delicate and tender feeling, responded like the violin to the hand of the master. On the occasion of her first communion she wrote a letter to her father and mother declaring her intention of correcting her faults expressed in a pious manner at which it is possible her parents, slightly affected by religion themselves, may have given a tolerant smile. In the midst of her sorrow, when she was twenty-two, she wrote in a little book she had used in the convent, which she kept to the last day of her life: "Precious souvenir of my youth, companion and guide of the holy hours which are passed for me, remind me always of the grand and solemn ceremonies of the convent chapel".

At eighteen, Clotilde left the convent and returned home. The education she had received had been slight; she loved poetry and had a deep feeling for music but had received no instruction in it. Later we find she shared Comte's feeling against "conventual establishments" for education, and not long before her death she planned an article on the abuse of scholastic institutions.

She was of a gay and joyous disposition, loving to tease her brothers, and dancing with delight, and with her pale auburn hair and delicate colouring was a vision of hope and gladness in the home of the Maries. She was happy to be at home again and her love and admiration for her mother influenced the development of her mind, for Madame Marie, daughter as she was of the high and exclusive nobility of Lorraine was largely emancipated in religion, liberal in politics, and devoted to the poor. She discussed with her daughter her views of fraternity and the bond between them was very close.

This happy joyous period lasted but a short time for Clotilde, owing to her parents' anxiety to establish her suitably in life. A year after her return home Amadie de Vaux was appointed as deputy to Captain Marie. He belonged to a family of noble origin, much looked up to in that part of the country. It may be that Clotilde's mother liked the idea of her daughter's returning to the class she had herself forsaken by her marriage; she had certainly experienced poverty and hardship. However this may be, the parents, unfortunately, planned a marriage between Amadie de Vaux and Clotilde and as they had no money to provide her with a dowry they decided that Captain Marie should resign in de Vaux's favour if the marriage took place. Then they would only have the trousseau to provide.

de Vaux was thirty years of age and of a kindly disposition. Clotilde accepted the arrangement of her parents although both they and she doubted whether Amadie had strength of character. The mother had even remarked on his selfishness but at this time marriage was almost the only resource for a young girl and there seemed much in his favour. Writing to Clotilde later of her effect upon him at this time, he says:

> " I loved you, not perhaps with a passionate, but with a pure and sweet love; you charmed me, and I thought you beautiful. I knew you to be so pure, so beautifully brought up, you seemed as an angel to me ".

After the marriage Clotilde strove to attach herself to her husband and to carry out the duties of a wife, but she never felt love for him and the hope of respecting him gradually diminished. Still, neither she nor her parents had any idea of the tragedy which was hanging over them. A year after the marriage M. de Vaux was appointed to the office of Captain Marie who resigned.

A year later a child was born who died immediately, Clotilde herself being very ill indeed. Something of the intensity of her sorrow and disappointment we can guess, for although before the child was born she doubted whether she wished for it, we hear later that the desire of her heart was maternity. The loss of her child partly revealed to her the intensity of her own feelings.

Three years after her marriage, while she was visiting at the home of her husband's brother, Amadie de Vaux decamped burning the papers at the Tax Office, which was broken into by the authorities to find a heap of ashes instead of the documents. Amadie was a gambler and had used the sums he had collected as tax gatherer and now escaped. He was never captured nor did his wife ever see him again. All their things were seized, even her wardrobe, and the unfortunate girl had to take refuge at her parents' house without even a hat or mantle just in the dress she had on.

The family of the Maries had prided themselves not only on their honour but on that which Clotilde called better, their honesty. Captain Marie's term of office had been marked by honourable conduct in every way and this disgrace was very painful indeed to them, they were also impoverished for Captain Marie had given up his post that the husband of his dear daughter might be provided for.

The Duc del Ficquelmont, her mother's brother, offered Clotilde a home in his family, for the two families had long been reconciled, but this Clotilde gratefully declined; she had already decided what she would do. If she became a member of the family of an aristocrat she would lose her personal independence, and she wished to dedicate herself to social reform. As her thoughts dwelt on all she had suffered her great desire was that others should not suffer in the same way. She found herself, a beautiful young woman barely twenty-four, chained for life to a man who, were he found, was doomed to the galleys. She decided that, while trying to steel her heart from any affection, which could only be gratified by disorder, she would write something which would call attention to this cruel anomaly and save other women from such a life, for, although where there had been true love no moral failure or crime should cause it to fail, where, as was then the custom in France, a woman was given to a man, without choice of her own, she should not be bound to wear out her life in loneliness for one socially dead to whom her heart had never been given.

Clotilde's family were disturbed at her decision, perhaps they felt that she was not sufficiently educated for a literary career, and feared the difficulties and temptations of an independent life. Her uncle, apparently not offended by her refusal to live with him, paid a small sum every year to help in her maintenance and her mother added something to this. We do not know when she gave up her Catholic faith but probably when she wrote the inscription in her little book she was beginning to lose it and she became completely emancipated. She was in fact the ideal modern woman, desiring mental independence and freedom from the trammels of mere convention, fearless in examining the foundations of belief and rules of conduct, and fully determined to carry out her convictions and devote her ripening powers to social service. To this she added the charm and grace of the old regime and the humility which was the result of her early training in the worship of the Madonna.

For two years she lived with her parents and found a dear friend in a married cousin, then she went to Paris and lived with her brother Maximilien until his marriage, afterwards she had a small apartment of her own in the Rue Payenne 5 near her family. In a letter to her brother, written in 1841, she says:

> "Oh do not do away with the family. It is true it has its defects of organisation but it has something which no other society has, a true interest in every one of its members, and the inexhaustible consolation which the love of a mother gives . . . I love mamma with all the religion which the great virtues of her heart inspire and I can truly say that I never answered her with impatience or ill humour without regretting it bitterly".

Clotilde de Vaux had yet to undergo a fiery trial, the worst she experienced. She met a man (who it was is a secret buried in Père La Chaise) a man who responded to all the noblest feelings and desires of her heart. She learned to love him with entire devotion and intensity. He responded with equal ardour and evidently begged her to accept the home and life of love which was her ideal of happiness, but they were separated by a double obstacle, her unhappy marriage, and his bond, which she found included duties. She strove to transform her love into a sisterly or maternal tenderness but all in vain, her heart was torn by passionate feeling, her health was undermined. At last she determined to separate herself from the man she loved and to see him no more; only then, she says, she began to live again. It was a painful life to which she returned, every night she asked herself should she have courage to live another day, sombre thoughts of suicide passed through her mind but were successfully combated. How her path became clear to her at this time and how she was sustained during it, we shall find explained in her novelette " Lucie " which was written in 1843.

This book has little resemblance to the English novel, it is rather the descendant of such writers as St. Pierre, Madame de la Fayette, Madame de Staël and other French writers who have analysed delicate feeling. Like the " Princesse de Clèves " and " Delphine " it is autobiographical and might have been named like Goethe's story " The Confessions of a Beautiful Soul ".

We have seen that the old sanctions of society had broken down, free unions were usual and in such a case as Clotilde's would have been considered by many not only justifiable but desirable. She herself was entirely emancipated, Hell had no terrors, Heaven no attraction for her, nor did she trouble about her personal dignity, she would have sacrificed herself willingly for love, mere convention had no power over her, and she had the passionate desire for maternity, but her deep love of others, her strong altruism, so enlightened her mind that she was able to disentangle the human sanctions of conduct from theologic and conventional sanctions. In other words, she realised the meaning of positive morality through her spontaneous worship of Humanity.

Lucie, like herself, is the young wife of a man socially dead but her husband has been transported for life for robbery and murder and her lover Maurice is bound by no ties. He tries with respectful tenderness to induce her to form a union with him and as they were resting outside a little church when a marriage party came out he called her attention to their look of happiness. " Oh my beloved ", she said, " they are happy but it is because their happiness offends no one ". " Maurice our unhappiness must not drive us against society, its institutions are great and admirable through the efforts of the past. It is unworthy of noble souls to spread around them the sorrows they have to bear ". Personal happiness must not be bought by cheapening the moral attainments of the race which are the heritage of all. For human beings social service implies loyalty to society. Only by legitimate means must they try to alter the conditions so that others may not suffer as they have done.

She tells her friend how she could have devoted

herself to Maurice and describes the simple joys and duties of family life with a longing affection, and cries, " What pleasures can surpass those of devotion ". The reputation of Maurice is dearer to her than her own happiness, and when they must part she begs him to leave her the consoling thought that he will—

> " pour out upon society the floods of devotion and love that are within him ". " Generous feelings are delightful to experience ". " What destiny can be grander or sweeter than that of a man who is useful in his generation ".

Clotilde had also written much poetry but she destroyed it nearly all as not worth preserving. We have only two poems of hers, a few lines to childhood, called " Innocence " and the charming lyric or "canzone', as Comte called it, "The Thoughts of a Flower ". This has been ably translated into English but, as is the case of so much French poetry, the elusive charm cannot be caught in another language. It has the beautiful fetichistic expression characteristic of true art.

Such was Clotilde de Vaux when she and Auguste Comte met, he, the man, the philosopher, who had by steady labour and profound insight carried the positive spirit and method up to sociology, and she, the woman, the artist, who had by the depth of her feeling carried it into the highest region of all, personal morality.

CHAPTER VIII

" The Year of Years "

THEY met for the first time at the end of 1844, but they already knew something of each other. To Madame de Vaux Comte was the eminent thinker and philosopher who had recognised her brother's merit and whom her brother revered, and Comte already knew a little, and soon learned more, of her sorrows and of her refusal of a life of luxury and dependence.

In the following April their intimacy began. The year from this time until the April of 1846, when Madame de Vaux died, has been called the " year of years ", the " peerless year ", the " year without compare ", a year of gradually deepening affection and of mutual understanding and appreciation. Although they were constantly meeting, one hundred and eighty letters were exchanged between them, wonderful letters marked by perfect candour, their inner thoughts and temptations, their hopes and their aspirations are acknowledged with a transparent sincerity seldom to be found.

The friendship affected them very differently.

To Clotilde, still occupied with her sorrow and with her voluntary separation from the man she loved, it was a solace and an inspiration. In her first letter she writes: " I hope that your beautiful and noble teachings may sometimes find their way into my heart and mind "; but in the heart and mind of Auguste Comte it wrought a revolution which was almost terrible. A great and noble love coming for the first time to a man in his maturity, like maternity to a mature woman, has an intensity unknown to youth, and Comte loved Clotilde with this passionate intensity. It was a new birth for him, upon his starved and lonely heart this new sweet feeling fell like rain upon the parched land, and awakened new life within him. He knew what this would mean to his work, it had come at the right moment. Through weary years he had struggled on and laid the foundation for the regeneration he had foreseen, now the new impulse would enable him to fulfil his remaining task with a deeper knowledge of human life and love.

The strain as he began to realise this was great and his health was upset. He could not sleep, and his illness in 1826 recurred to his memory. Sophie, his faithful servant, who had tended him with silent sympathy all through the time of his separation from his wife, thought it was this that was still troubling him and redoubled her care and attention.

In May he told Clotilde of his feeling for her; her answer was sad, she had hoped that their friendship would have led to their happiness, she suffered in the thought that it was not so, she begged him to put aside such thoughts. He promised to try and transform his feelings, speaking of the noble re-awakening she had given to his desire for moral regeneration. She consented to continue the friendship if he would avoid embarrassing subjects and wrote: " I should reproach myself all my life if I brought trouble to a sensitive heart ".

On the day of St. Clotilde, Madame de Vaux's fête, he sent her as an offering his " Letter on Social Commemoration ", in which he pointed out how the positive doctrine will appeal to women because it puts moral teaching above political agitation. He was anxious to show her that far from being irreligious positivism embodies all past religions. The cherishing of memories is one of the most important of religious observances uniting the past, present, and future. In antiquity it reached apotheosis, but could not be extended to the lower castes. The beatification of catholicism was a great advance as it was bestowed on the poor as well as on the powerful, on St. Geneviève as well as St. Clotilde. In positivism it will be perfected by periodically recalling the memory of the worthy and in drawing them from all classes, races and beliefs. Every type of human character will be honoured, catholicism was too narrow for this, not even admitting all of its own noble examples. The effect of baptismal names will also re-appear for it springs from the tendency of human nature to venerate noble types, and to take them as models.

Positivism does not come to destroy, its object is to construct, and it combines into one harmonious whole all that the past offers of the grand or of the useful. Everywhere it separates the fundamental purpose from the passing form in which it was clothed. The earlier systems pass away as their power of protecting the social truths of which they were the confused expression fails. Real or positive conceptions as they gain ground will be found better adapted than fictitious to noble human purposes.

Feeling the depth of his affection, Clotilde told him in her next letter of the state of her heart and that never under any circumstances could she be more to him than a sister.

It was a severe blow to Comte to learn that the heart he longed to win was already given to another but he was deeply touched by the confidence she had shown him, he will not give up their friendship but he will transform his feeling and he will redouble his love for Humanity.

Returning her confidence he told her of his period of insanity.

He then refers to her writing, for all through this year of deep personal emotion neither of them forgot the work to which both had dedicated their lives. He advises her about her literary career: " Never let that degenerate into a trade (métier) which ought only to result from spontaneous inspiration "; and he warns her not to develop her talent at the expense of truth and purity. He had no doubt heard that in " Lucie ", which was just being published, she upheld divorce. He told her how his own experience would have led him to desire divorce but he had seen its social harm, and then he adds:

> " Humanity is in travail for total regeneration, may you have the noble ambition to second her worthily instead of blindly hindering her ".

When he wrote again he had read " Lucie ", and had seen how entirely it was written with the noble ambition of which he had spoken, the ambition to second Humanity worthily by upholding the social bonds she had created through the love and labour of so many generations. The divorce Clotilde desired, he found, was only in those extreme cases when the continuance of the bond would almost necessarily lead to social disorder. He told her that the relative nature of the positive philosophy, " opposed to all absolute rules," would admit exceptions in such cases.

As Comte read and re-read " Lucie " and realised how much of the life of Clotilde it represented his love for her developed more and more towards adoring veneration. He saw that this charming and graceful woman, when she was little more than a girl, had, by the strength of her heart and the depth of her altruism, divined the human sanction for personal morality: " What pleasures can surpass those of loving service." Here was shown the identity of duty and happiness. The whole spirit of " Lucie " embodied the motto he later adopted for positivism: " Live for others." It was born in upon his mind that the motive power for social regeneration was love. Thought was but its minister and servant.

Looking back upon his own past he saw it was his love for mankind which had led to his life's work, without it all his mental power would not have availed, and as he dwelt on the past he felt how little he had understood the social meaning of personal conduct. He thought of his mother, Rosalie, who had striven to train him in right conduct, and how he had thrown aside her teaching, and in doing so had brought about the misery of his own life, how he had helped to degrade still further the downtrodden victims of civilisation, he thought of Pauline and the hearth he had desecrated, the husband he had dishonoured, how his own marriage had been carried out in defiance of the wishes and feelings of those he should have considered; as he thought of these things he felt unworthy of her who had revealed true love to him in his later days, he was " convicted of sin." The apostle of truth who had begun to appreciate beauty became the apostle of goodness.

The vision, blinding him for the moment by its intensity, as in the case of St. Paul, helped him to see more clearly for the rest of his life. The full nature of Humanity was gradually revealed to him. He saw that the influence Rosalie had upon his childhood was of the same nature as that which Clotilde had on his maturity, together it formed the human morality tending to repress selfish feelings and develop tenderness and consideration for others. He had deliberately put himself under the opposite influence, he had followed Duessa and the love which led downwards, and cast aside that of Una which would have " imparadised " his soul.

So his maturer thought began to take shape and the means by which the collective action of Humanity is brought about, which later he defines so clearly, was made manifest.

He wrote to Clotilde in August: " My growth in universal love has increased under the constant stimulus of our pure affection ". From the day of St. Clotilde his love had been purified:

> " Let us hope my Clotilde that this sincere fraternal affection may beautify all the remainder of our private life, at the same time, it will, I am sure, make the whole of our public life more perfect ". " To you alone I dare speak freely of all the developments concerning the moral grandeur of man of which I have dreamed."

" Lucie " was published in the " National " and an offer was made to Madame de Vaux to become a regular contributor. Comte dreaded the effect of journalistic writing on her especially as Marrast, whom he distrusted, was the editor.

At this time she planned her novel "Wilhelmine" in which the heroine was to " strike upon all the shoals of passion still preserving her purity and was gradually to reach the fulness of family life ". " I try to keep her pure of heart while erratic in mind because I am reserving her for a work of wisdom she will accomplish under the new philosophic direction ", later, she says that she only means to " make her a philosopher in heart, loving Humanity without fear of Hell or hope of Heaven".

" What I understand best in the 19th century is the universal tendency of people to simple good sense. Seeing how the mind can derive the benefit of all discovery naturally and without effort I see more clearly every day that science only needs to be at the head of society to enrich it throughout, and so I console myself for not having learned the wonders of the square of the hypotenuse ".

Both were endeavouring to advance in their public work by the help of their tranquillised affection. But a severe storm lay before them; Clotilde, full of admiration for the noble philosopher who had honoured her with his friendship and adoration, pierced to the heart by the thought of his loneliness and suffering, dreading that his preoccupation with her would delay his work, and also, no doubt, impelled by the desire of maternity, the one personal feeling which was strong within her, suddenly decided to do as he wished, to accept his protection and all the duties of family life.

The rapture with which Comte received the letter containing this decision can be imagined, to her, to whom he had already owed the " purest and sublimest emotion " of his life, he will now owe " unhoped for happiness " in that part of his life when he had expected " awful loneliness ". Is there the faintest trace of disappointment that the idol should step down from the pedestal? For the first time there is in both a thought of caution and concealment. However this may be, it is lost in the shock Comte received from a letter written three days later in which Clotilde withdrew her offer. Even in a letter written between the two she speaks of him as " her tender father " shewing how little her feeling corresponded to the suggested relationship between them.

In those three days Clotilde, the modern woman, had made the great discovery, a discovery impossible before the emancipation of woman, which came when she was able to give herself instead of being given. Clotilde found that she could not give herself without love. She had discovered that the crime between the sexes was the giving oneself without love.

Striving towards this truth Shelley was persecuted and his character blackened in the conventional time of George III in England. For no cause should man or woman give themselves without love, not even the desire of maternity which had prevailed with so many women can justify it. For mutual reverent love should precede maternity and should make the atmosphere about the growing child be he the result of the marriage or the child of adoption. To the sanction which society gives this inner sanctity must be added to create a true marriage.

The difficult question of divorce would settle itself if the hearts of men and women inclined to keep this law, for even if some aberration came to one of the pair in such a marriage, the memory of true love would make the innocent one desire to help and save the guilty. Clotilde, her Lucie, and Comte had all given themselves without love, the two former from the circumstances of the time when Dante's words did not apply to woman:

> " Libero, dritto, e sano è tuo arbitrio
> e fallo fora non fare a suo senno
> per ch'io te sopra te corona e mitrio "
>
> (Purgatorio 27).

and the latter by his own act. These then were typical of the unhappy marriages which were the result.

The heart of Clotilde had again led her right and guided her to the highest personal morality. " All marriages ", she wrote later, " where there is only consent on one side end unhappily, perfect agreement is necessary for true love ".

The unconscious recognition of this truth has often led artists to choose the irregular union where this love existed as more typical of the true marriage bond than the loveless marriage. So Dante in the Middle Age and Watts in the 19th century chose the story of Paolo and Francesca to shew the union which neither Pain nor Death, no nor even Sin nor Hell could sever.

It is very evident that at the time Comte would not be able to see it in this light. He felt Clotilde's withdrawal bitterly and for a moment regarded it as feminine caprice, but his veneration for her almost immediately induced him to accept her decision and he wrote on the tenth: " I resume then without effort my dear habits of chivalrous tenderness ". From this time the letters express their growing attachment, his shewing increasing devotion and hers a deepening admiration and tenderness.

Her letters abound in delicate and charming expressions, shewing her consideration for others and her desire to make the best of the actual human beings around her, which had such an effect on Comte's after life, softening the harshness of his judgments, and developing the sympathy which became so marked in his later years. One of her expressions is: " the evil drug fault finding " ; another: " Our race more than others requires duties to develop feelings ".

After the crisis between them she told him more of her past suffering and added: " I have understood better than anyone the weakness of our nature when it is not directed to a lofty aim beyond the reach of our passions ". Although worn out with the struggle of life she feels she can teach others and says " that remains a real interest in my life ".

He rejoiced in her determination to work and trembled whether he should remain worthy of one who in the midst of anarchy had devoted herself to spreading the moral lessons she had learned in her own life.

In November Clotilde wrote: " I look upon myself as so much surrounded by your honourable and holy protection that I shall regard you with the simplicity and confidence of a child ", and, in another letter, she says he has been able " to revive a fainting soul and pour balm into a fainting heart ".

In December he wrote to her:

> " Instead of forgetting our differences of sex let us by common consent put this to its noblest purpose, the mutual improvement of our nature both intellectual and affective ".

And she wrote to him:

> " I place you with all my heart upon the pedestal you are raising for me, it better becomes you than me ". " May I be able to prove to you better than by words my affection, esteem and respect. Whatever be our fate I hope that death alone will break the bond founded upon these feelings ".

In January she wrote:

> " I raise you above my daily troubles like a banner destined to overcome them, a true attachment is the finest emblem to display before the enemy ".

Clotilde continued her novel in spite of the increasing difficulties of ill-health; she asked Comte to write her something about marriage from the Positive point of view to include in it and he responded by the fine " Philosophical letter on Marriage " which is published with his works. In it he traced the development of marriage through its earlier stages, and pointed out that the new philosophy would carry it to higher perfection and develop it to finer issues. Clotilde read it with keen interest and in the letter of thanks uses the expression: " We all have one foot in the air over the threshold of truth ". In February she wrote:

> " Souls full of scruples and ardour meet with many a Golgotha in this world but at least they often escape regret and remorse ".

The devotion between the two intensified, Clotilde however, insisting on the necessity of her independence both in heart and conduct, she must not be doubted or controlled, she claims complete trust.

Comte was never tired of expressing his gratitude to her for the regeneration she had wrought in his life. He did little this year but it was truly a case of " reculer pour mieux sauter " for all his future work was influenced by this " peerless year ". He had many anxieties, as his letters to Mill shew, his means of existence were precarious, the three Englishmen were not prepared to continue their contributions and he had to seek lessons again. But all these things were as nothing, he was so occupied with the love in his heart.

Their increasing attachment was not looked upon with favour by Madame Marie and her son Maximilien and this led to increasing friction which, unfortunately, became acute as the life of Clotilde drew towards its end. The ardent feeling of Comte and his anxiety for her health which he did not think they sufficiently considered, made him appropriate her in a way displeasing to them and, greatly as he admired her desire for harmony, his nature was not yet sufficiently disciplined to enable him to bear with them.

In her last letter written on the 8th of March Clotilde wrote:

> " Your affection makes me very happy and sometimes very thoughtful, I cannot help thinking that some day you will reproach me with these violent distractions affecting your public life . . . You make a mistake when you say there is no love in friendship . . . . . If we could both talk calmly I would prove to you that friendship can be loving and brave, that is why I honour our attachment by all the sweetest and holiest names I can find ".

Comte had begged her to accept the services of Sophie during her illness and a deep attachment grew up between them. Sophie had an adoring feeling for this charming and gifted woman who depended upon her in her weakness and she served her with that self forgetting devotion which is found nowhere in greater perfection than in the domestic relation; and Clotilde clung to her in confiding trust. They became sisters in heart, and this friendship was an earnest of the entire disappearance of class feeling amongst women, whose work is essentially the same, that of creating, educating and tending the children of the future.

It was in Sophie's sympathetic ear that Clotilde breathed her tender confession that Auguste Comte had at last won her complete affection and that her heart was wholly his. Sophie listened sadly as she talked of the happiness which lay before " we three ", for she knew that Clotilde's days were numbered. Still, she rejoiced that she would have the satisfaction of telling Comte that this supreme gift was his, and she watched and tended her with unwearying care for eighteen nights until the last hour drew nigh; then Clotilde said to Comte with loving pity: " You will not have had your companion long ". " Comte ", she said later, " Remember I have suffered without having deserved it ", and then this " beautiful soul " passed into the land of memory and gratitude.

Who can picture the grief of Comte! The pent up feelings of a life-time were concentrated on her. She was his all, he had not then realised what Sophie would become to him. He knew she was a " perfect servant " but could not guess she would become to him a daughter and faithful disciple. The whole treasure of his heart was in Clotilde and she was no more.

Two things saved him, his social mission always present to his mind, and the fact that she was now associated with him in that mission. It was for him to make her worth known to the world, for now he knew that for the foundation of the religion of Humanity, for the comprehension of that social being made up of men and women, man alone was not sufficient; the intimate and complete co-operation of the sexes was necessary. Now the two were summed up in his brain it was for him to carry on their joint work. Beatrice had inspired Dante throughout his life by the young vision of her beauty and purity, Clotilde's influence would never pass away from his life, and she was not only an inspirer, like Beatrice, but also an active co-operator; had she not been the first to perceive the human sanction for personal morality?

With brave heart and determined courage he turned again to his life's work.

CHAPTER IX

Desolation and Dedication

"We meet again
within the minds of men"
—Shelley, Revolt of Islam.

HE began at once to organise his inner life so that Clotilde should be always with him and then, a week after her death, he decided to recommence the "Positive Polity" adding to it a chapter, "The General View", and to write the Dedication to Clotilde which he had planned in her lifetime. He had nerved himself immediately to receive a visit from George Henry Lewes which had been arranged before. He wrote to Mrs. Austin who was again in Paris, telling her of his loss and pointing out how the new philosophy reconciled the needs of the heart and mind. With his letter he sent a copy of "Lucie". Mrs. Austin, having read it replied: "Alas! we can see too well the sufferings of a noble and tender soul, one sees also a clear and lofty mind which has been able to surmount its own hopes, regarding them as exceptional, not affecting the important rules of life. Few of us attain this rare merit; I regret her for you and for myself, she would have been a precious friend for me. She is to be envied".

He wrote to his friend Mill telling him of Clotilde's death and of the loss it was to the world, as in spite of her own unhappy experience she had decided, on his suggestion, to devote her literary powers to upholding the sanctity of marriage attacked in the writings of a great Frenchwoman of the day. He told him also, in answer to Mill's enquiries, of his straitened circumstances and that the slight economy he had planned of moving into a smaller apartment would be too painful now as the memories of the visits of his beloved friend were connected with his present home. He had need of such sympathy as his friend could give for there was much to try him apart from his absorbing sorrow. Madame Marie and Maximilen refused to let him have the MS. of Wilhelmine which Clotilde had promised to him on her death-bed. Captain Marie, her father, opposed their action in this matter but his opposition was of no avail and, as a matter of fact, this MS. still remains in the Marie family.

On the first visit to the grave of Clotilde he had striven to lay aside all irritation. These visits, and his times of communing with her, were no mere indulgence in sentiment. He had set himself the task of becoming like her, he had seen her constant consideration for others, her scrupulous respect for the family, and her attempt to make the best of all around, and the remaining eleven years of his life were one long effort to incorporate her nature in his own.

We have seen him as the hero pursuing his task

through almost impossible conditions, allowing neither domestic misery, poverty, nor terrible illness to turn him aside; as the sage gathering all the knowledge of the past into one harmonious whole, now he began the gradual ascent which was to make him one of the greatest of saints. He had been stern and harsh in judgment, even suspicious in his relations with his own family and with the Maries. He had accused his sister and the Maximilien Maries of mercenary views. With regard to Alix, he may have had some experience, of which we know nothing, but certainly Madame Maximilien Marie, who tenderly and reverently cherished the memory of Clotilde through so many years, keeping a vivid picture in her mind of her sweet beauty, showed herself pure in heart.

Indeed, how could he have been a saint at this time, the asceticism and self-torture of a St. Simon Stylites may be attained in solitude but the qualities which make the human saint do not flourish untended in the heart. In the words of Madame de Staël, who was as truly the spiritual predecessor of Clotilde as Condorcet was of Comte:

> " L'âme qui n'a jamais connu le bonheur ne peut être parfaitement bonne et douce. Si je conserve encore quelque sécheresse dans le caractère, c'est à ces années de douleur que je la dois ".

He was a man of forty-eight years and for thirty-nine of those years he had lived without the happy family life in which acts of loving service become self-fulfilment rather than self-denial. His firm determination to endure his wife's infidelity and importunity, and not to expect tenderness, was discipline—perhaps, but rather tended to isolation and spiritual pride than to the growth of sympathy. The wonder rather is that directly he came in contact with Clotilde's truly human nature he recognised its beauty and made it the model of his life. He saw what was needed for the completion of his task.

Like Christian, he stumbled in ascending the Hill Difficulty; he had to go down into the Valley of Humiliation before he reached the Land of Beulah and the Celestial City. He shewed in his own life the inner meaning of prayer, he carried to Clotilde's grave, at his weekly visits, and to his daily communing with her, all his sorrows, hopes and joys; trying everything by the test of his ideal, he resembled it more and more.

It was born in upon his heart how much he owed to his mother Rosalie; it had been her early training which had left its effects and had enabled him to respond, so long after, to a similar influence. Rosalie planted, Clotilde watered, and Humanity gave the increase.

In May, he recommenced his free public course on astronomy, prefacing it with some introductory lectures on the general spirit of positivism. At one of these lectures he said: "I hope a public demonstration in favour of Jeanne d'Arc will soon replace the shameful glorification of Bonaparte". He paused, doubting how this would be received as Bonaparte was the popular idol, but to his surprise there was a storm of applause beyond anything that had ever been given him before. It was led by an old workman.

His large audience, partly composed of Parisian workmen, appreciated him and it was their custom to thank him warmly at the end of each course. Here, in the following year, 1847, dealing with the influence of women at the time of the year at which Clotilde had died, and feeling the sympathy of his audience, he was led on to speak of her, of her influence on positivism and of his own loss. He was listened to with respectful sympathy and even deep emotion. As the audience went quietly out a fashionably dressed man spoke loudly and coarsely of the incident, upon which a working man, usually one of the most silent, reproved him with indignant irony shrugging his shoulders contemptuously. A low murmur of approval followed this reproof and the fine gentleman slunk away. The hearts of the Parisian workmen rang true and responded to genuine feeling.

At the end of this course he proclaimed the dogma of Humanity amidst the respectful attention of these same workmen :

" Humanity the only true great being, whose necessary members we are, concentrating always upon Her our thoughts that we may know Her, our affections that we may love Her, and our actions that we may serve Her ".

The death of Clotilde was followed shortly by the death of a friend Charles Bonnin who although an old man had become one of his devoted followers, and by the news that his father had been deprived of his post as public cashier. He resolved to try and heal the breach between himself and his family and wrote expressing his sympathy. Unfortunately, he did not mention his sister, and on his father's resenting this the reconciliation fell through. Although there were other attempts, the final reconciliation only took place two years before his death.

He had been cheered a few days after his loss by a letter from Holland signed by three engineer officers speaking of their admiration of his work, which they considered completed that of Bacon and Descartes, and enclosing a copy of a Dutch translation of the first two chapters of the " Positive Philosophy ". It helped him to be assured at this moment that the " Philosophy " was already spreading into the countries of Europe.

In the autumn he wrote the Dedication to Madame de Vaux, perhaps the noblest prose elegy ever penned. In it the social point of view is ever present, he speaks of the universal progress towards perfection being in both of them the principal aim. Both had felt that feeling must be supreme, not hampering but giving direction to the intellect, but she had helped him to realise this more fully, through her he had experienced the re-action of pure personal love on philosophic thought. They had both felt the necessity of the union of the sexes in the regeneration of mankind. As in the individual nothing can come without harmony between the mind and heart, so all social improvement needs the co-operation of man and woman:

" Both of us clearly understood this beautiful adjustment of functions related and independent". " between two services so indispensable there could be no question of preference ".

" The highest purpose of our union was to make our hearts more perfect and that purpose can still be pursued with delight, even though the intercourse of feeling is active on one side only ".

" If a whole life hardly suffices for two beings to know and love each other thoroughly why should death break off the continuity of sympathy ".

" Henceforth I give myself exclusively to the noble civic passion which from earliest youth devoted every energy of my being to the great work of regeneration ".

" Your silent aid cannot be taken from me, during our sacred year of happiness your sweet impulse mingled, far more than you could ever believe, with my highest philosophic inspirations. The same blest influence has been with me the last six months, aiding my thoughts as they moved onwards in the midst of tears. Wisely cherished it will continue to purify and kindle my highest thoughts ".

" Farewell loved pupil, true fellow-worker! Thy angel influence will govern what remains to me of life, whether public or private, ever urging me onwards towards perfection, purifying feelings, enlarging thought and ennobling conduct ".

"Thus only can thy benefits now be recognised, by rendering my own performance of the mighty task before me more complete".

The Dedication of which these few extracts may give some idea was completed on the 4th of October, the anniversary of the day on which Clotilde had given him a lock of her hair which they called "Le don du coeur". During this year Comte also made several preliminary attempts at the Table of the Soul or Psycho-Analytic Table, the perfected form of which has been given at the head of the 3rd chapter.

His constant religious musings revealed to him the personal nature of the instincts of race preservation both sexual and maternal and gradually purified his desires.

He was passing through a time of material difficulty. His means were so straitened that the payment of the allowance to Madame Comte was delayed. This distressed him, as he had been most scrupulous towards her in this respect. In January, 1847, he received a letter from her threatening to return to him if the allowance were not paid, he answered sternly, that if ever she made this attempt he should apply for a legal separation, assuring her at the same time that as soon as possible the money should be paid.

In this letter he told her of his relationship with Clotilde. Wishing she should know before it became public he had asked two friends to tell her but neither had found courage to do so, he now said that, painful as it was to tell her this, he felt it right that she should know it.

In spite of all attempts to repress and silence him he was becoming known and a body of enthusiastic disciples were drawing round him. Among these was the young Pierre Laffitte whose affectionate nature and quick intellect was a real solace to him. Three evenings a week Laffitte visited the master, eagerly drinking in his teaching. Sometimes they went for long country walks when Comte would pour out his grand ideas in eloquent words to the delight of his pupil, for his conversational powers were extraordinarily brilliant, and, sustained as they were by his intense faith and wide knowledge, enthralled his hearers. Once when he was in the full flow of eloquence a little child ran up to him and asked him the time, interrupting the current of his thoughts. When the child was gone Laffitte expressed his annoyance but Comte with one of his rare tender smiles pointed out that the child had paid him a compliment, had practically expressed his confidence in him.

There is another anecdote that one day a friend complained that his literary style was too heavy, and asked if he could not lighten it, upon which he answered: "My friend, my work is to make wholesome bread for the people. If I wanted to make meringues do you suppose I could not do it"?

A later saying, which must have been told by the man to whom it was said, is of graver import. Comte, stopping one day at a book-stall, saw a young man, to whom he was attached, reading a book which he saw was a prurient novel. Putting his hand affectionately on his shoulder, " How long my friend ", he said, " will you commit self-abuse on your brain?

Owing to Laffitte's sympathy he was able to tell him much of his sorrow in the loss of Clotilde. Laffitte expressed his belief that some day a grateful posterity would bury them in a common grave. After this Comte took him to the sacred spot where she lay and pointed out a neighbouring place where he wished to be buried, and it was here that his sorrowing disciples laid him eleven years later.

But an even more intimate and cherished help was vouchsafed him. Sophie, the " perfect servant ", shared in his adoring love for Clotilde, and they constantly spoke of her together, he was led on to speak of his hopes for the world and gradually the loving heart and strong intelligence of this simply nurtured woman made her one of his most convinced and devoted disciples. At the time of the Revolution of 1848 she said " Philosophers should brave arms without carrying them ". About that time Comte took her husband and son to live with him that Sophie might have the full happiness of family life, he blamed himself that he had not thought of this before, pointing out how much easier it is to think of oneself than of others; but his constant worship of the type of tenderness and purity was rapidly softening his whole nature and he was creating loving bonds with all around him.

Later he adopted Sophie as his daughter and she watched over him with tender care until his death.

CHAPTER X

Reconstruction

THE Revolution of 1848 had long been foreseen by Comte, he saw that a constitutional monarchy was entirely unsuited to the genius of the French people who had been accustomed to consider the king personally responsible for the action of the government. The middle class ministries of the reign of Louis Philippe had retained much that was undesirable from the old imperial days, they gave titles, crosses and epaulets, they copied the English parliamentary system but limited the power of voting to the owners of property, refusing to allow the formation of trade unions or public meetings for the free discussion of opinion. They had no settled policy except their desire for peace. The people had been promised security of employment with wages sufficient to bring up a family and provide for rest in old age so they now wanted the right to unite to enable them to attain what had been promised; the indifference of the governing classes turned them towards communism.

At the time of this revolution the Republicans were divided into three groups composed of, first, the conservatives who wished to keep the rule of the middle class, replacing the king by an elected president, second, the socialists, who wanted to do away with central administration, to destroy the army, confiscate the endowment of churches and impose their reorganisation at once by law and, third, the little band of men united under Comte in the Positivist Society who recognised social law, that the present must grow out of the past, and that free scope should be given to the natural development of the State. To maintain order in the midst of disorder was the task of statesmen.

The Positivist Society met in Comte's Apartment and appointed committees to report upon the different questions occupying public attention. Magnin, a workman, drew up the report on the labour problem which advised that, while waiting for the regeneration of opinion, government should intervene to diminish the most crying evils, to encourage wiser and more disinterested actions among the chiefs and to uphold industry which was the basis of the future order. Littré drew up the report on the form of government, which advised that it should be republican with the device of "Order and Progress", that there should be an elected Dictator who could be deposed and replaced in case of need, that the budget should finally be under the control of the leaders of industry but should for a time be entrusted to a triumvirate of eminent working-men, that the army should be reduced and transformed into police, that the church and university endowments should be abolished and people left free to decide whether theology, metaphysics or positivism should be the basis of the spiritual power, and that the past should be glorified. To meet this last need, Comte published his historic calendar in which men of many countries who have taken part in the Western transition are honoured.

Comte's followers were not listened to, their leader had long been subjected to what has been called the "conspiracy of silence". They were mostly young workmen who continued to meet during Comte's life, but their numbers were much diminished after Napoleon's coup d'état in 1851 when Comte counselled the acceptance of the new government as an accomplished fact trusting that Napoleon would keep his word and respect the Republic. The word of the Napoleons proved as little to be depended upon as that of the English Stuarts and when Napoleon re-established the Empire Comte expressed strong disapprobation.

Comte's old enemy Arago was appointed to an important position, and being convinced that he had written too harshly of Arago and hoping now to strengthen his hands Comte made a public apology which led to a sympathetic touch with his father and sister who approved of his action. His sister wrote: "It needs a great courage and a noble heart to say in public that one has been wrong".

Arago never acknowledged the apology and continued his animosity as shown by the fact that Comte was still passed over in the appointments at the Polytechnic, although he was on two occasions put first on the list by Poinsot whose business it was to choose the most suitable candidates for the appointments. His free lectures for the Parisian workmen were also stopped on the pretext that no hall could be found for them!

He wished to seize the moment of the Revolution to publish his " General View of Positivism ", for it was by change of opinion not by law that harmony could be attained:

> " Written laws do not create social order but only preserve it when it has been created ".

But he was destitute, how could he print the " General View " from which he expected so much? Three Dutch disciples came to the rescue and paid for the publication. Comte felt it contained the germ of the religion of Humanity which would not be lost to the world even if death should now put an end to his labours.

His situation was desperate and he feared he would have to give up the beloved home and perhaps even sell the furniture so connected with his past. Again help came at the time of need. Sophie had for some time begged to be allowed to lend him her savings and she now insisted and her husband seconded her wish, the six hundred francs she had saved were placed at his disposal, a sacred trust in his eyes of which the grace and devotion were constantly before him. Then his landlord granted him delay more than once for the payment of his rent. These things could have been but a passing help had not Littré decided to institute a fund to which those who valued his teaching or pitied him for the persecution to which he had been subjected, might subscribe. Comte in speaking of it describes it as:

> "the spontaneous inauguration of republican manners, the new chivalry, which will paralyse dangerous oppression".

For three years from this time at mid-day on Sunday he preached the religion of Humanity at the Palais Royal to an audience of women, students and workmen, eloquently recalling the whole of the past, unfolding the progress of the future, and then, returning to the present, pointing out the path of social advance. Many young men became earnest positivists and the name of the Master was honoured but the Press still remained silent.

Among the letters written at this period is one to Williamson, professor at the London University College, in which, after speaking with approval of much of his letter and especially of the axiom, "Everyone has enough benevolence to wish he had more", he points out his errors. Williamson had suggested that Paris would be the centre of the Spiritual Power and London of the Temporal, and that England would rule the rest of mankind. Comte replied that such an opinion could not exist outside England, that he was exaggerating collective differences which tended to disappear while individual differences tended to increase. With civilisation each country would more completely represent Humanity. Also that the Temporal Power allows of no one centre, it is local, and its concentration would mean tyranny and a struggle between London and Paris, resembling that between Rome and Germany in the Middle Ages. Industry tends to the dispersion of centres, whereas science unites. Peace and the removal of all tariff prohibitions will dispose each nation to the industry best suited to her condition. The spiritual power was not local, and England should not give up her share in it to which her glorious past entitled her.

He urged one young friend who had just lost his father to surround his mother with care and consideration, telling him he had failed in this himself and would not like him to suffer from the self-reproach he had had to bear.

Another he urged to be open with his parents as to his opinions, telling them reverently and trusting to their consideration, " untruthfulness ", he added, " and weakness heal nothing ".

To his beloved young friend Laffitte, he poured out his hopes in many letters, and discussed with him the houses and the possessions of the workmen, the future arrangements and the government of France, the education of the people and the establishment of the religion, " the coming of the religion as bringing an era of true repose of heart and mind a truly normal state towards which all the other states were but preparations ".

At this time he hoped that Laffitte would be capable of being his successor. He considered him mentally efficient and told him of the two meanings of the word Heart; he did not lack tenderness but was deficient in energy or, in other words, while his heart and mind were fit, character was lacking, and he urged him to strengthen this in every way. There was real sympathy between them, as he expressed a thought Laffette seized it at once sometimes completing it before he had done so himself.

In another letter he says that the duty of the Spiritual Power is to classify men by their moral worth, independently of rank, and this classification, he adds, prevails after death, which, instead of levelling all, brings out the personal inequalities sometimes hidden in life by outward circumstances. Equality is impossible, it is fraternity we need, and the greatest care should be taken in the use of language by those whose mission was reorganisation, he himself hoped always to deserve the reproach of "prudery" in philosophic language Mill once gave him. He longed to give to others the moral and mental ardour growing in his soul.

In another letter he speaks of substituting for the sanguinary banner of the Revolution the green banner of hope with the intellectual and moral mottoes, "Order and Progress" "Live for others".

At the time of his first spoliation in 1852 when the head of the Polytechnic wrote expressing his sympathy and indignation, Comte answered:

"The only political programme suited to our mental and moral harmony is to maintain order energetically, to support the industrial order wisely and always to respect the spiritual movement".

CHAPTER XI

The Main Building

THROUGH the devotion of Longchamp, who guaranteed the expense, the first volume of the "Polity" was published in 1851; it was the main building of which the "Philosophy" had been the foundation. Comte's whole nature had expanded since he wrote the "Philosophy" and this had reacted on his mental outlook.

The first volume consists of the Dedication already noticed, of the "General View", a bird's eye view of positivism, which had been published before, and an account of the abstract sciences. The object of the "Polity" was to reconstruct opinion for the regeneration first of Europe then of the world.

The SUBJECTIVE PRINCIPLE of the reconstruction was the subordination of the intellect to the heart. The OBJECTIVE BASIS: the external order of the world revealed by science. The discovery of law in social science satisfies the principle without danger to the basis. It follows that politics must be subordinated to morals for progress is the development of order.

The well-being of the people is the object of government. The leaders of industry will form the Temporal Power.

The formation of public opinion involves the acceptance of principles of social conduct and an organ to teach them. This will be the priesthood.

The united action of philosophers, women and the people is the moral or modifying influence in society. Woman's influence will be increased by the improvement of marriage which is tending towards complete monogamy.

There will be a wide field for art, in the construction of types and pictures of the future and past, in the organisation of the festivals idealising the different aspects of life and the commemoration of the dead. A doctrine encouraging man to strive for perfection necessarily encourages art. Ideal art is (after direct culture of feeling) the best help in our efforts to become more loving and noble.

He then deals with the sciences. Humanity depends on the external order and law is constancy amid variation. Natural philosophy is divided into cosmology and biology. Cosmology into laws accessible and inaccessible to human intervention. The inaccessible can be examined by inspection only and they give the first idea of natural order fostering submission, checking pride and vanity and promoting social feeling, by the consciousness of a fatality common to all. The accessible laws, which can be modified, develop energy.

The theory of the brain in biology gives clearness to the problem of human nature " to subordinate egoism to altruism ". This problem must be investigated in sociology since the solution lies in the power of the social state to develop the higher and repress the lower feelings, for moral unity can only be attained by the ascendency of social over personal feeling and practically it depends on social unity.

Religion is the combination of love and belief binding the man within and connecting him with the outer world. " Man grows more and more religious ". The history of religion is the history of man.

The second volume is on social statics, the fundamental order or constitution of any society whatever. Here he deals with the theory of religion, its object and history, with the family, the true unit of society, where each man and woman is trained by the constant stimulus of the social instincts; with capital on which every society depends for its continued existence ; with language by which its members communicate and the wisdom of the past is stored up for the benefit of the future; with the theory of social existence and with the limits of variation. All these subjects are treated exhaustively both as to their nature and history.

The third volume on social dynamics was published in 1853. It is on history or the development of the race. In this he traced the working of the law of the three stages through the whole past, bringing to bear upon it the scrupulous accuracy which Gibbon shewed in his study of the comparatively short period of the Fall of the Roman Empire, and the sense of continuous growth so remarkable in

Robertson's summary of the Middle Ages and to these he added the encyclopedic outlook and noble aim which were especially his own, these qualities he applies to the appreciation of every phase from the primitive savage to the time of the Revolution and unfolded with consummate skill the gradual advance of man under differing beliefs and conditions, each belief growing out of the preceding one and developing in Humanity in the same order as the corresponding phases develop in the life of the individual. History, he says later, must be regarded as " a series of preparations, in the inter-dependence of which lies their real utility ".

This volume alone would have been no mean achievement had it been the work of a lifetime. It has been described as the, almost too exciting sweep of the great past, and it is surely true that the growth of Humanity through the ages is the sublimest of all spectacles. Comte points out that these ideas were growing before his time, being careful to render honour to his predecessors.

Between the second and third volumes he published his " Catechism of Positive Religion " which was a summary of the larger work, intended especially for women and workmen.

The fourth volume, which may be described as a prophecy of the future of man as organised by the Religion of Humanity, was published in 1854. Such a prophecy, he warns us, cannot be exact.

By this time he had attained his full mental development, he had disentangled the highest science of all, that of morals, or of the individual from that of sociology. The table of the soul, the psycho-analytic table at the head of chapter III, he now saw as a part of the highest science. The full meaning of the religion of Humanity had dawned upon him, and in later days, he rejoiced that his main work was written after he had fully recognised science as a simple introduction to religion.

The religion of Humanity, he shews us, takes possession of the future as well as of the past, and those who teach must be competent for this important task; they have to reconcile order and progress, the East and the West. All the religions of the past have been only parts of the religion of Humanity which incorporates them all; the completeness of theocracy, the scientific method of Greece, the social purpose of Rome, and the feeling of the Middle Ages.

Extending prevision to social concerns pre-supposes the innateness of social feelings, without this there would be constant uncertainty in the action of men. The innateness of benevolent feeling and the earth's motion are the bases, one subjective, the other objective, of the positive philosophy.

" Humanity is the continuous whole formed of the beings which converge " or work together to a common end. This includes all animals who have helped mankind.

The elements of Humanity are states and families, the agents individuals. She is subject to the law of growth and improvement, as the past clearly shews. She acts through individuals and the problem is to combine concert with independence; all action lies with the living but they depend upon and are governed by the past, and they necessarily labour for the future. Service is the privilege of the present but the excellence of Humanity is shewn by the dead, they indeed represent Her, but their influence is passed on by the living.

Positivism secures the supremacy of love without degrading the intellect, which crowns love. The reign of Humanity is a reign of love, and to have helped forward the life of the future is the subjective immortality which noble souls desire, this is the spiritual immortality cleansed from all that is material or personal.

Humanity acts, in the aggregate, by four Providences: Moral, Intellectual, Material and General. The first is, generally speaking, exercised by women, who, by the education of children, and by their influence in family life, develop feeling and train to right conduct. To do this more perfectly they must be independent, that is, they should not have to earn their own livelihood, and they should have the highest education to be able to intervene wisely in public matters.

This judgment of Comte on the nature of women's influence has been strikingly justified by the very feminists who opposed his teaching. In almost all cases their intervention in public life has been to protect the oppressed or to give advantages to the downtrodden, more and more they have insisted on the importance of motherhood. In Finland, the first results of giving votes to women were the teaching of domestic duties in the schools and the sending delegates to other countries to find the best method of improvement in these matters.

The Intellectual Providence consists of all teachers, preachers, artists and men of science and, properly organised in the future, will bring the best teaching to every child, no more will education be the privilege of the wealthy, but all spiritual and intellectual treasures will be at the service of the people. The Intellectual Power, like the Moral, must be independent that it may never prostitute its gifts as a means of livelihood. Its members will resume the medical duties once in their hands as the mutual re-action of body and mind are fully recognised.

The Material Providence is represented by the industrial concerns, headed by the Capitalists who will recognise that the capital has been entrusted to them by Humanity to use for the benefit of their fellows.

The General Providence is composed of the mass of the people to which all belong when they are not exercising their special functions, and the work of this Providence is to oversee the others, to supply what is needed in each case, and to form the body of public opinion without which all teaching, law or sentiment is vain.

Comte then gives his forecast of the worship of the future. It is the idealisation of life, for only when we have idealised it within can we worthily realise it without. The future on earth is all important in the social religion. We worship Humanity to serve her better and the best preparation is the development of the sympathetic feelings.

By dwelling on the virtues and perfections of others we incorporate them in ourselves, especially when the possessors have passed through the purification of death, beautifully symbolised, in the West by the waters of oblivion and the river restoring the memory of the good, and in the East, by the gradual perfecting of the Buddha. This truth is evident in the private worship where every worshipper dwells upon the memory of those who have helped him in his life, types which will generally be drawn from the nearest ; how few there are who do not spontaneously worship the memory of the mother.

The domestic worship consists in the preparation of each member of the household to take part in public life by the consecration of each stage of his private career, men being dedicated to the simplest labour, as Kings and Priests have been in the past.

Finally, he sets forth the noble scheme of Public Worship by which, in the course of festivals (of which we see many spontaneous beginnings to-day), every relationship of human life, every phase of the past and the organisation of the future is honoured, so that each child of man shall, by the idealisation of life, be prepared to enter it fittingly.

One practical improvement for life and worship he instituted, the perfecting of the calendar by dividing the year into thirteen months of equal length with one extra day at the end of each year, and one in addition at the end of every four years, thus he carried on the work of Julius Caesar and Gregory. This has often been suggested of late, another instance of how much he was before his time.

The idealisation of the work of the capitalist and the workman, the consecration of both, and the instruction in their mutual duties by a body of men devoted to the teaching of all, seems a fair and beautiful picture in the midst of the present disorder, fear and resentment, but it is based on the gradual development of the past from slavery, through serfage, to free and independent labour, and its realisation lies in the not far distant future.

Every relationship is idealised in this comprehensive worship, for " Love is the principle ", the moving force in the social life of man.

The science which constitutes the doctrine of the religion is abstract but images must be united to signs, as when geometric forms are pictured on the inner space.

The First Philosophy consists of the universal principles which are the foundation of all ordered thought and apply to all sciences, they relate partly to the world and partly to the mind of men.

Dealing with the scale of the sciences, Comte insisted more strongly than before on the truth that all study leads up to, and culminates in, morals, or the study of man, each science developing his mind by its methods as well as improving his circumstances by its means. The end of science is right conduct, which depends, in the first place, on right feeling. This chapter forms the gradual transition from feeling to activity, the mission of the Intellect.

The next chapter " The Life " is a picture of the happier future when men of intellectual power will not vie with each other to sell their mental goods in the highest market but will accept simple conditions and devote themselves to the education of the people; the mothers in all ranks, having received the higher education, will be able to guide their children.

The Spiritual power appeals to feeling and reason, the Temporal is only concerned with acts. Personal, domestic and civic morality are parts of one process which consists in developing the higher instincts, rather than directly repressing the lower; the type to be attained is that of the mother's love who finds higher joy in ministering to her child than in a more purely personal gratification. Attachment makes the little child desire to share some delicacy with brother, sister or dog, and makes " giving up " a pleasure in after years. Veneration impels the strong man to protect the old and to curb his pride and vanity. Sympathy or Humanity makes all enter into the sufferings and joys of others putting their more selfish feelings aside, and in these cases it is not the loss of personal gratification that is felt but the joy of exercising the higher and nobler instinct, also innate ; it is not " sacrifice " but " fulfilment ".

The perfect family life will be more nearly attained in the settled existence, each workman owning his own house, which will become a sanctuary, enshrining the memory of the love and care of mother and wife, while the growth towards complete monogamy will hallow and perfect marriage. The necessity of a link between the Family and Humanity, to train feeling with reality and firmness through Patriotism, will lead to the development of small states where the love of the country can be realised in its intensity, all attempts of one country to seize and rule another, on whatever pretext, being regarded much as robbery by individuals is regarded to-day. All states will be united by common education and the worship of Humanity, the Spiritual Power extending its influence over all. The life of man is one and the aim should be to bring the tenderness, mutual consideration and trust, shewn in the family, to bear upon civic life and finally on international relations. Striving to approximate his conduct to the type of motherhood the employer of industry will, by sympathetic insight, understand the needs of his workmen and will desire to satisfy them when possible. More and more the Family, where the highest qualities are more intensely developed, will become the type of conduct to the citizens in their sonship to Humanity. The Rulers of society will undertake no work which is harmful to the race. The industrial era fully inaugurated and the idea of empire a dream of the Past, there will be no need for arms or other engines of destruction. Society governed by its leading citizens will be organised to useful ends. Honour will be given to capacity, while the hereditary titles and privileges will pass away. The aim will not be confined to family or country, but the good of all will be considered, the different virtues of the white, yellow and black races recognised and incorporated.

The strong will devote themselves to the service of the weak and will receive in return respect and veneration. Capital will be transmitted with function to the successor, and workmen will renounce all resort to violence, confining their action to non-co-operation in cases of tyranny. Wages will be paid to the workmen in two portions, one fixed, sufficient for the maintenance of his family, the other variable, according to the results of his labour. All work will be paid at nearly the same rate, a slight difference for town and country but the equality extending to all countries. Wages, stipends, salaries are not the price of labour which has no money equivalent, but are conditions and means of action.

The government will be in the hands of the three most capable administrators of capital, the ministers for agriculture, manufacture and commerce, these ministers will give their services gratuitously. All people having received the same education, will meet in the salons of the women and discuss public matters. Class distinctions in society will have passed away, the only distinction will be between command and obedience so essential in industry. Tenderness will be extended to the very small portion of the human race to whom steady work is an impossibility. They will not be shut up but will be maintained with kindly feeling as mendicants, from whatever section of society they have come.

Uniformity in all countries in the laws of marriage and inheritance, in coinage, weights and measures, and a common language, in addition to the local one, will greatly facilitate intercourse between the peoples.

Each country will produce the products suited to its soil and climate, thus avoiding waste. The condition of man's kind and faithful helpers, the animals, will be improved and the heaviest work given to inorganic forces.

Nor will the Earth herself be forgotten, here also there will be no waste while care will be taken to avoid unsightliness and to develop the beauty of the planet. Reverencing the products of human labour men will learn to respect the materials which make such products possible. The wisdom of man is condensed in this law: " The noblest order perfects the lowest by submission to it ".

Under the guidance of Love, under the control of Faith, Action unites and strengthens the union of the two, by the development of collective industry.

In the last chapter, " The Transition ", the (probable) steps are traced by which the new construction will replace the old and the order in which the different nations of the three races will adopt Positivism. Paris will be the centre during the transition but in the normal state the centre will be found at a point uniting the East and the West.

In speaking of England he says that the ruling classes, " the ablest since the Roman Senate ", are capable of conducting the change without revolution and " may have the unparalleled honour of directing, in an orderly movement the formation and installation of the normal state ", but he warns them, they must act quickly or the élite of the British workmen will outstrip them and place in power the successors of Cromwell. If the Patricians do not " to their eternal honour, to the great good of the people and even of the whole world, avail themselves to the full, of the more striking advantage of their position ", the revolution in England wll be more stormy than elsewhere.

One act of poetic justice he proposed, that Oceana, with suitable compensation, should be given to the black race as a sin offering from the West.

In conclusion he points out that foresight is the result of the dependence of our inner life on the outer world. An astronomical calculation shows a coincidence between the chain of thought within and the succession of events without, so, when extended to the social order, true harmony is attained, the picture within corresponds to the reality without and man's mind becomes the mirror of the world, and the picture deduced from the past helps him to understand and regulate the present.

As the work had been preceded by the Dedication it was now followed by an " Invocation " of the beloved friend in which he traces the seven steps in his advance which he owed to her influence, the stimulation to higher and more complete thought which had been the result of their intercourse. The first was the realisation of Humanity, not as an intellectual construction but as a composite Being, feeling, thinking and acting: the one life in which the many found their fulfilment. The second was the formation of Positive logic by the adoption of the subjective method that is, the method of sympathy. Logic includes Feelings, Images and Signs, and Clotilde had helped him to realise that feeling alone can combine images with signs to elaborate thought. The third was his construction of the cerebral theory (the psycho-analytic table) ; The fourth was giving the highest place to morals, thus placing the religious construction higher than the philosophic creation. The fifth, the separation of the spiritual and temporal powers. The sixth, was the connection between the two extremes of man's initiation, fetichism and positivism, uniting the whole history of man. Clotilde had shown her complete sympathy with both ends of the scale by her charming fetichist poem, "The Thoughts of a Flower", and her novel "Lucie", a positive idealisation. The seventh step results from the others and from appreciation of human life. The worship must be before the doctrine even as in life love precedes and is a necessary condition of understanding or knowledge.

Thus her subjective influence had helped him, she had, as he said, "renewed the light of the intellect by the flame of the heart", but he felt how much more quickly he would have advanced had he been blessed with her presence. Indeed, it is difficult to estimate the loss to the world which her early death has been. Her constant presence, when he had, as he intended, adopted her as his daughter and the happiness it would have brought him would in all probability have prolonged his life, and the effect of her nature on his disciples, the women she would have brought in, all these things might have made a great difference in the advance of the religion.

CHAPTER XII

The Loving Philosopher

HE had accomplished the task he had planned in early youth but his life's work was by no means at an end. He had long seen the necessity of a third work to consist of the reconstruction of the abstract sciences from a central or synthetic point of view. He intended to write the beginning, on mathematics, and the ending, on morals, himself, leaving the intermediate sciences for later followers who should be especially skilled in them.

Before beginning this "Subjective Synthesis" he would pause for a year as was his custom after finishing one of his undertakings. Such pauses were necessary, as when he began to write he wrote straight on, without alteration, everything being arranged in his mind before he began.

There was much minor work done during this year of leisure. Since Littré had established the fund for his maintenance, Comte had written a circular each year, to be sent to each contributor, in which he pointed out the value of such a fund; as it freed the thinker from oppression and enabled him to devote his life to important work. He looked upon it as the beginning of a Sacerdotal Fund by means of which capable young men, showing themselves disinterested by renouncing wealth, might be trained to teach the people. For himself he was proud of such an effort made on his behalf and would have been more so if the sum had been raised by subscriptions of a centime a day, contributed by working men. He was strict with those who undertook to subscribe, it was a duty which must be regularly carried out and the amount should be in proportion to income. For some years the sum subscribed did not reach the minimum, but before he died he had the satisfaction of seeing it passed, and some devoted disciples, notably the Dutch group, made it up to a sufficient sum in the early years. When it passed the 7000 francs considered necessary he would not take more for himself. He accounted to the subscribers for every penny of his expenditure, his one extravagance was, he said, his apartment which was larger than he required but Sophie was an excellent economist and the food for both did not cost more than fifty pounds a year.

During this year of comparative leisure he wrote his " Appeal to Conservatives ", a short treatise addressed to the governing classes. The term " conservative " was not applied in France then, as it is in England, to a political party, it had been used as the name of a periodical put forward by the men who honestly tried to combine order and progress, men like Lamennais, one of them, who often discussed with Comte the regeneration they both desired. These conservatives or " constructives " are men, of any class, who while reverencing the past and striving to be worthy of its traditions, are yet alive to the future and to the progress needed to unite the two harmoniously. Such men there are, men of wealth, who, living simply themselves, try to improve the conditions of labour, do not ostentatiously head large subscriptions but have quietly formed themselves into the modern chivalry ever ready to succour the distressed, and behind them there is a large body of workmen who have no illusions about wealth, but only ask for such conditions as shall enable them to bring up their children in happy homes and to give them an education which will enable them to share in the intellectual and spiritual treasures of the race. To all such men Comte made his appeal to help forward the public programme of Positivism even if they did not understand its doctrines. For certainly such men would approve of the meaning of Positive, that the aim should be reality and usefulness, that it should not be vague and wandering, but certain and precisely understood, that it should be organic and capable of growth, and relative, and finally that it should be morally sympathetic. He urged them then to put feeling first, morals or right conduct to be the aim of all effort intellectual or practical, to make it relative to the needs of the time, to bring about the separation of command and counsel, with complete liberty of speech and opinion, to maintain the dignity of women and improve marriage; the family being the school of tender feeling where selfishness was lessened, not by conscious repression, but by the growth of love, and to ennoble the family by making its object the service of the city; to help forward the growth of patriotism by gradually dividing the overgrown empires and to ennoble civic life by subordinating it in its turn to the wider bond in Humanity.

Such true conservatives would convince the reactionists that the order they loved would not be subverted but would be developed by the very progress they feared, and would make clear to the communists that the altruism they desired would prevail better by utilising the institutions of the past than by destroying them.

He also wrote his Will although he hoped to live, having planned work for many years to come. With complete trust in the devotion of his followers he directed that the sacerdotal fund should be kept up, the allowance he had given to his wife paid, the apartment kept as a meeting place for positivists, Sophie to be its guardian and to receive a pension, the books and many other things to be the property of his successor. His followers justified his faith and as far as was possible carried out his Will when the time came.

They had a difficult task, for the shadow which had darkened his life was not removed after death. Madame Comte had hoped to regain her influence over him, she attended his lectures and he wondered whether she now appreciated the doctrine she had before slighted. He felt he would value the adhesion of one so intellectually distinguished, he treated her with courtesy, ordered an armchair to be brought for her when she appeared, answered her letters, but firmly declined any personal interviews. When a hall was denied him she intervened and obtained it by her influence and he said she had gained the gratitude of all Positivists, but when she tried to force further intimacy and began to revive old grievances which could only lead to recrimination he put an end to the correspondence. From this time her action became more hostile, and she spoke scandalously of Comte's relations with Madame de Vaux and even with Sophie. Then all the chivalry of his nature, which had for so many years sheltered her, was turned from her to the protection of those two so dearly loved, so reverently cherished, and he made a confidential disclosure to Sophie of his wife's history that she might be able to protect herself after his death. Telling Dr. Robinet he had done this (but without telling him what he had disclosed) Dr. Robinet persuaded him also to write a secret codicil to his Will. He did this, directing that it should be destroyed if Madame Comte died before him and that it was only to be used in case of need. It may be doubted whether, had he consulted his inward guide only, this would have been done.

On his death Madame Comte refused all the conditions of his Will, occupied the apartment and sold his things alleging that she did so to pay his debts, not regarding the express arrangement he had made about debts. It is not surprising that a proud woman should persist in this attitude when threatened with the secret codicil by the executors.

She who had been a complete unbeliever all her

life disputed the Will on the ground that her husband was a madman and an atheist. His things were put up to auction, the garments well worn in the service of Humanity were exposed to the mockery of the curious and the profane. His disciples rallied to carry out his wishes, bought back his things and secured the apartment where all was replaced reverently and in due order by the loving hands of Sophie.

At the time he made his Will five days were devoted to his writing, one to correspondence, every Wednesday he visited the grave of Clotilde and on Saturday morning spent half-an-hour in meditation in the Church of St. Paul, Rue St. Antoine, where the ceremony of baptism had been performed when Comte and Madame de Vaux were sponsors for her brother's child and which he regarded as the beginning of their spiritual union.

On Wednesday evening the Positivist Society met in his rooms, and one evening was devoted to Pierre Laffitte whom he still hoped to appoint as his successor, other evenings he received visitors from seven to nine, when he charmed all by his conversation. Those who knew his habits left at nine. He had been prepared to give up his home if necessary but it would have been a bitter blow to him, for he could work there better than anywhere else. It was full of the memories which helped him, there he had had the great relief of finishing his Philosophy, which circumstances had made so heavy a task, there he had gathered his band of disciples round him and there above all Clotilde had visited him.

In addition to his intense feeling and strong and clear reasoning he was gifted with extraordinary powers of imagination, equalled only perhaps by William Blake and some of the mystics of the Middle Ages, and the mystics were helped by the belief that the visions they summoned up had an actual existence outside of them, while Comte knew well that they were the result of his own will and imagination. He could gather his disciples around him when they were far away, he took pains to find out the features and costumes of the great types of history and reproduced them at will, thus he could always be in noble human surroundings, and for his beloved colleague he vividly recalled every look, every expression, every attitude, he lived in her presence, he remembered every word from the days when she sat in the chair, so sacred to him now, and held the conversations of which we can form some idea from the Catechism.

Where can a parallel be found to these two in their short year of intimacy, the ardent lover and the woman growing in tenderness towards him, discussing the future of man and the glory of Humanity! All must rejoice that he was allowed to retain the home which held these memories for him. The last years of his life were the happiest for he had experienced the joy of a pure and noble love and he had by long and sustained effort disciplined his personal desires and had advanced far on the path to perfection.

He had become the living witness of the power of the religion of Humanity which he had shewn to the world, for who, seeing the change in him, could doubt the efficacy of positivist prayer. It has been said that prayer is useless, even a mockery, unless there is some outside power consciously hearing it. On the other hand it is pointed out that prayer has been answered whether addressed to a so-called false god or true one, and that the earnest setting of the heart towards ideal beauty and goodness has always been the cause of improvement. But no argument of this kind can equal the effect of the sight of the growth in gentleness and saintliness of this man who had thrown off all early training and been harsh and arbitrary.

There are many accounts of him at this time written by different disciples.

He had, as we know, thought himself without charm, he was called ugly, with one weak and drooping eye, and was subject to nervous contortions, but such was the mastery of the soul over the body that, as he spoke, the power and brilliance of his glance was astonishing and his hearers were carried away by the charm of his conversation which was sometimes gay, with sarcastic touches, causing the amusement of all, but when he spoke of the religion and of the regeneration of the world they felt themselves in the presence of a saint.

He had many disappointments, for his powers fascinated men and they seemed to understand him and agree with his views when they were really carried away by the charm of his personality, then, later, when he found their ignorance he thought they were faithless and traitors to the truths which they had accepted. These thought him harsh and despotic. He was so intellectually truthful himself that he could not understand the vagueness and uncertainty of some minds, but even towards such men he became more tolerant for he carried all his difficulties, all his hopes and failures into the ideal presence of Clotilde, and strove to attain her courteous gentleness and consideration for all; how he attained this the words of his followers will shew. An Irish disciple writes:

> " He impressed me as a man deeply in earnest, convinced that he had by his genius and life-long labours reached the central truth of morals and religion. He inspired confidence by his constant efforts to correct his own faults ".

James Hamilton, his English pupil, who had at first regarded him as a precise, severe and unsympathetic tutor but who had gradually realised the higher meaning of his teaching and the deep feeling that lay beneath, visited him at intervals and says of him, in 1851:

> " I was able to remark the wonderful change which had come over the expression. . . He now reminded me of one of those mediaeval pictures which represent St. Francis wedded to Poverty. There was a mildness in those attenuated features which might be called ideal rather than human ".

and his beloved physician Robinet speaking of his influence, says:

> "It was shewn even more in those private interviews which he kindly gave every day for the moral needs of those who approached him. No one could make himself with more generosity and charm "all things to all men". It was in these moments of sweet and beneficial intercourse that he gave counsel and private direction with power and love; his words at these sacred moments have saved many from doubt, from weakness and irresolution, from the torment and danger of revolutionary malady, from moral death and the devouring leprosy of egoism. . . And many can witness that whenever they approached this noble man they left his presence better, wiser and more resolute".

For he was now not only the philosophic teacher, the Founder of a school, but the spiritual Father, tender and wise, the moral guide of his disciples whom he regarded as his children, the first minister and priest of the Human Religion which he had made known to the world. The title he liked best was that of "The Loving Philosopher".

CHAPTER XIII

The Master and his Disciples

DURING the last years of his life Comte's correspondence greatly increased and by no means the least valuable part of his work is found in the mass of letters he wrote. Men of eminence sought in him not only the intellectual guide but also a moral teacher. Many who had never seen him found help in their personal and family difficulties as well as clear guidance in matters of thought. The number of subjects touched on in these letters is very varied, ranging from the right way of teaching Latin to children to the temporal and spiritual government of mankind in the future. He expected much from his disciples for he was no quietist, the result of the most devout meditation was, in his own case and must be in theirs, stimulation of social ardour. Guided by Positivist principles they should at once devote themselves to social regeneration each one in his own place and according to the needs of his surroundings should be the earnest apostle of the new order. His heart had room for them all, he taught, exhorted, reproved and sometimes, with intense suffering to himself, renounced them, he says:

" Spiritual fathers even more than natural fathers are subject to the fate of loving more than they are loved."

He entered into and considered their difficulties and duties were they English, Dutch, German, Italian, Spanish, Brazilian, American or French. He was anxious that all should have the international honour of their country at heart, it was for the people of each land to see that their country did nothing unworthy in the comity of nations. He had advocated the return of Algeria to the Arabs by France, and he wished all the nations of the West to return the spoils they had taken in other lands. He urged his English followers to remonstrate against the " injurious anomaly " of Gibralter. Cobden had already suggested its restitution at a meeting of British merchants, and Dr. Richard Congreve, who became the first public apostle of Positivism in England, responding to Comte's appeal wrote his able essay " Gibraltar ", which met the master's cordial approval. He hoped this work would stimulate feeling in Germany in favour of Italy. In each country the natives themselves should repair the wrongs, for this, true patriotism was necessary, the step between love of the family and love of Humanity but " since the end of the Middle Ages the western peoples have had no real country owing to the enormous size of the political aggregations. The only patriotism which has developed during the period is that of the English and this has been marred by the exploitation of the rest of Humanity" and then he adds: " Since the invasion of France in the 14th century until the shameful opium war in China in 1841 the British power has been the most disturbing in terrestrial affairs ". But when a disciple feared that in India, Egypt and China there might be destruction as there was in Mexico, Comte tells him there is no fear of this, " their social existence is too firm " and he was sure that the nobler souls in England would disavow the attack on Canton which had excited these fears:

> " We shall soon find a spontaneous support for the moral effect of positivism in external relations, since the voice of the English themselves will be raised, with an increasing energy, against the oppression in India ".

The Crimean war had been undertaken as " a war against war " but had degenerated into an offensive war, and he blamed the siege of Sebastopol, for although the Russian Empire must break up, it was not for those nations " which will assuredly meet the same fate " to bring it about by violence. It is a general truth that war excites such evil passions, such unmeasured hate, that even when undertaken from noble motives it ends in an orgy of cruelty and destruction.

He says: The English Revolution, radically greater than the French because it was religious and led by two of England's greatest sons whose apotheosis he hoped to live to see in the Panthéon, was shamefully misunderstood. Danton alone in the

French crisis approached Cromwell in the nobility of his social aims. If the continuity of the two Revolutions could be shewn the sympathies of the British workmen would be brought out towards the French.

He had many contacts with England. We have seen how Mill and Lewes honoured him though they could not follow him in his later work. His influence can be plainly seen in the novels of George Eliot who became a positivist and whose finest poetry " The Choir Invisible " and passages in the " Spanish Gypsy " and the " Minor Prophet " are expressions of positivist doctrine. Sir David Brewster speaks of Comte's Philosophy as " profound science conspicuous for the highest attributes of intellectual power ", and notices " his simple yet powerful eloquence . . . his enthusiastic admiration of intellectual superiority, his accuracy as an historian, his honesty as a judge and his absolute freedom from personal and national feelings ". In 1853, Harriet Martineau translated and condensed his " Philosophy ". This work delighted him so much that he recommended it should be read instead of the original and he told her in a letter that he was struck by the " extraordinary insight due to the heart no less than the mind by which you have so deeply felt the social destination of a philosophic composition of which most masculine judges have only realised the intellectual tendency ". The authoress had, indeed, so entered into the spirit of his work, and realised its social meaning, that, dry as the work might seem to some, she had translated parts of it with tears in her eyes and these were passages which Comte had written with deep emotion; yet, in later years when he re-read his early work, he felt it so lacking, compared to the stage he had then reached, that he said, with the humour which underlay his intense seriousness, that he was obliged to read a canto of Ariosto at once to take the taste out of his mouth!

Miss Martineau insisted on sending him part of the profit she had made on the book, he could not accept this for himself as he had renounced all profit from his writings but it was used to pay the cost of printing his works.

He calls attention to the importance of making the distinction between republicans and revolutionaries quite clear. The retrogrades and the revolutionaries approach each other and will finally coincide when " the profound affinity between anarchy and reaction shall be better understood ". It was our lot in England, in 1926, to see this affinity illustrated when both the diehards and the communists were ready to fly to force while the mass of the working men, even during the terrible suffering of the lockout, shewed extraordinary self-control and strove to preserve peace.

Comte urged his English disciples to less reserve, to shew more sympathy with men of other races, this lack of " élan " is " the radical vice of British souls " and he found this even in the Irish group who, he says, were English settlers. They must be brave and patriotic: " It would be strange if boldness belonged only to men without mind and heart ". He realised that Dr. Ingram's position, a professor under Anglican domination, made it impossible for him to speak out and says that official professors should confine themselves to perfecting the teaching confided to them, without introducing misplaced propaganda, but he probably did not know that Dr. Ingram was the young author of the national song " Who fears to speak of 98 " which rang through Ireland stirring all hearts. In later life the tender feeling shewn in his sonnets to his dead wife would have touched the heart of the Master, and when he retired in old age he made his profession of faith in the religion of Humanity. He had fine intellectual gifts and it was said of him at the time of his death that he was perhaps the most learned man in Europe. On another disciple, Henry Dix Hutton, Comte impressed the need of veneration and moral culture too much neglected. It is owing to the habits of submission learned in the Middle Ages that the western peoples have accepted scientific truths which could never have passed into universal circulation if insubordination had always existed. The revolutionary state in practical life is " that every one aims at ruling while no one wishes to obey " and in matters of theory " Everyone pretends to teach while no one wants to learn " " without veneration nothing can be learned or even enjoyed, stability of mind or heart cannot be attained in morals or sociology or even in geometry or arithmetic. It is not enough discipline to accept those truths which have been demonstrated, for the laws of the mind make this inevitable: " The faith must always be demonstrable but it cannot always be demonstrated ". " Veneration ", he says, " is the sign of the elect ".

Comte was encouraged when practical men adopted positivism and tried to put it into practice, he advised Winstanly, a wealthy young Englishman, to plan the improved cottages he was building in the French or Italian style, rather than the English, which meant social isolation for the agricultural labourer. Hadery, a Frenchman, tried to make his farm labourers into one family, living as simply himself as they had to do. He felt that the most important question of the day was the " incorporation of the proletariat into society " and that the most powerful means to this end lay in the improvement of the working men themselves. Comte agreed and wrote that it was first for them to moralise wealth:

> " When their opinions and habits are rectified it will be easy also to correct the wealthy who will then be pushed from below by an irresistible force and from above by philosophic teaching".

But philosophic teaching will be in vain

> " while working men secretly aim at the very same idleness and pleasures which they blame in the rich ".

They must realise the dignity of labour, and Hadery's task was to develop in them the feelings and customs which would turn them from dreaming of the middle class as the only desirable end of their career. No better work could be done than thus to help by special practice " the holy social theory ". Also he must be ready for political activity, for all eminent practical men ought to be ready to help their dear country.

To a barrister he says there is still important work to be done at the bar but that cases should only be undertaken after they have been carefully considered and proved good, he warned him against the habit of the profession of deliberating without concluding. He warned the young banker Deullin not to neglect his special work in his interest in social progress:

> " I hope positivism will help you to appreciate your noble profession more completely and to perfect it by purging it from all gambling, enlarging it by worthy investments and ennobling it by wise and generous patronage ".

Bankers are the generals of modern industry. It pleased him to hear that Deullin was meditating on the sociological appreciation of the Bank but when he suggested a central Bank Comte replied it would have a bad effect as the Temporal Power should not be centralised. On the other hand he warned him not to be so immersed in his work as to lose interest in larger questions as this leads to moral and social degeneration, and to the young Dr. Fisher, who had pleaded his own absorption in his examinations as an excuse for not writing, he answers:

> " Man should dominate all his occupations not be dominated by them ".

Such absorption is a sign of weakness, special work must be harmonised with social interest. Social harmony would be endangered if men gave up public interest as well as if they failed in their special work:

> " Private worship can never be developed and kept up unless the need for each practice has been felt, daily duties interfere unless there is scrupulous regularity "

and the same applies to correspondence which then becomes a form of worship. To the Vice Attorney General at Bordeaux he says that the duty of a positivist magistrate is to know how to " sympathise with backward souls ". An Italian sent him a paper called, " Solution of the chief problems which agitate our century ". This was in complete agreement with the feeling and thought of Comte's own work and he hailed it as a proof of the preparedness of Italy for the new order. She might pass directly from catholicism to positivism without French deism or German pantheism. Italian would be the universal language because it was best adapted to art and poetry and had not at that time been oppressively imposed on other countries. The best minds in Italy were ready but they needed positivism or he feared they might fall under an oppression which would make the larger part of the population regret the Austrian yoke. One disciple he advised to seek the society of women and workmen for they are the elements of the moral force which is to regulate the world:

> "The modern renovation will proceed from below even more than it did in the times of St. Paul and St. Bernard".

But these two classes must be aided by the intellectual power, his own glorious mission had been to constitute the moral, after having shewn the mental, superiority of the new religion.

Any sign of overcoming class distinctions gave him hope and he was delighted when Dr. Robinet's wife wrote a tender letter to Sophie and they asked her to be the sponsor for their little child. About the same time an American disciple named his child Sophie Clotilde shewing that at this time the beauty of the bond between the three was recognised. To a disciple who wrote to him in physical and moral difficulties he gave encouragement and advice and advanced his theory of the chaste marriage in cases where physical or mental conditions make it undesirable that children should be born. The beauty and the helpfulness of such unions could be completed by adoption. Thus he deals with the subject of birth control, now so much before the public, but in how different a spirit to much of the modern teaching. It is by the gradual growth of self-control and a more ideal relation between the sexes that this will be brought about, not by the acceptance of a lower standard. To another he explained the value of the vow of widowhood in the positivist marriage, a good influence is purified and ennobled by death, the subjective life must be developed, all idea of the objective or conscious life after death being given up.

To those who ask advice about their health he suggests a sober and regular diet without wine or other stimulants but in a case where a questioner has already carried self-discipline to the extreme Comte advises the opposite, more food and even wine, playfully reminding him that if he is to "live for others" he must live and not die, and remarking that even the celebrated Dr. Sangrado, in spite of his praise of water, had wine in his pharmacopœia! His principal advice for health was the attainment of unity by benevolent feeling. A morbid condition is often the lack of some great social enthusiasm, some absorbing influence outside self:

> "only in an immense common destination can noble souls find harmony and happiness".

Physical and moral conditions and public and private life can only be appreciated together.

To Dr. Audiffrent, who was the most capable of truly comprehending and sharing his social and intellectual aspirations, and of whom he speaks as his "tenderest and most devoted disciple", he unfolded his theory of vital harmony which he would have dealt with at length in his book on Theoretic Morals had he lived to write it. Health is unity, or ease, the only disease is alteration of unity and this may be by excess or defect within or without:

"We are thus led in practice to the general consequences by which medicine and morals are related. Disease resulting from an alteration of unity, while unity rests essentially upon sympathy, it is rigorously demonstrated that the best way to keep oneself in health consists in developing good will. The gaiety, the security which the habit of living openly brings, guarantees health and happiness" . . . .

"While in the lower animals only the organism and milieu have to be considered, in man the former must be decomposed into individual and collective for it is through Humanity that the world dominates man and man modifies the world, its influence on the individual is indirect depending on the stage in the life of the race. Humanity protects man from the world as well as passes on its benefits".

An instance of this truth is, how different the effect of a thunder storm on the man cowering under the fear of the anger of an infuriated God and on him who, conscious of a lightning conductor, pursues his usual occupations tranquilly. The "isolated man" is an abstraction which is as vicious in medicine as in politics". Audiffrent posed the modern problem "To destroy disease, poverty and war". Comte accepted this but made the order war, poverty, disease, for poverty followed war and disease poverty. The problem is still unsolved (1927) and until the governments of the countries firmly decide against war, poverty and disease must be the lot of the governed.

Audiffrent, who became an able doctor, dreaded dissection of the human body and Comte answered him that the scientific imagination by which the interconnection of the parts was accurately and clearly pictured in the inner space, was of far more value than dissection but far rarer and more difficult to attain. Comte regarded the medical as the noblest profession and speaks of it as the "nursery of the new philosophers":

> "the general theory of the sympathies must come from a positivist doctor capable of understanding the influence of the brain upon the body without which doctors will be only bad veterinary surgeons".

and he speaks of the necessity of

> "the reaction of the heart over the mind to avoid the grave dangers of medical materialism".

For the last stage in development must be decomposed into scientific and philosophic. Science, though the necessary basis is not by itself fully positive, reality must be combined with utility in relation to Humanity.

Audiffrent's tender heart helped him to enter into the master's ideas even more, perhaps, than his unusual mental power. Through loving memory of a negress who had been his nurse he entered into Comte's feeling for the black race, he preached to workmen and tried to convert women, associating with the women of the people, but above all he appreciated from the first the share of Madame de Vaux in the formation of the religion. This was a constant joy to Comte, who felt that he owed his power over hearts to his adoration of her. His love of giving and receiving sympathy increased with the years and he delighted in the circle of disciples, now growing too numerous for him to gather them all consciously around him at sacred moments:

> "I have obtained more than I at first hoped since I am already, in my sixtieth year provided with a treasure of affection which I feel sure will be permanent".

He loved to gather them, in his mind, in his old home at Montpellier, and wrote:

> "This precious group, where my true family, both living and dead is clearly present to my heart, constitutes the best result of the whole of my career".

He had achieved, owing to his worship of Clotilde, empire over himself:

> "a wholesome discipline frees us from weariness, doubt and irresolution which unregulated souls have to endure".

Through his constant worship and profound meditation the law of the subjective life was revealed to him and, in a letter to Hadery, he utters the sublime truth that the type worshipped, whatever originally it may have been " gradually attains the filial type " even in the case of the mother " filia del tuo figlio ", for the attachment which originally established the loved one in the heart stimulates the veneration which reveals the noble and worshipful qualities and this in its turn develops the sympathy or benevolence which enables the lover to envisage the whole life of the beloved as the mother enters into the life of the child. Thus true worship results in the worshipper growing more and more in the likeness of Humanity. This was rapidly brought about in Comte's own case, for his adoring love for Clotilde was mixed with profound pity for the anxieties and sorrows of her young life, and his regret for all that he did not give his mother, Rosalie, filled his heart with a yearning pity that all she had lavished on him must have seemed to her in vain.

CHAPTER XIV

The Minaret

"So on our heels a fresh perfection treads,
A power more strong in beauty, born of us
And fated to excel us, as we pass
In glory that old darkness."

—Keats' Hyperion.

IN 1856 Comte published the first volume of the last important work he had planned, "The Subjective Synthesis", of which he was to write four volumes, the first on mathematics, the second and third on theoretic and practical morals, and the last on industry. Of these he only lived to write the first, of the second and third some indication had been left by the planning of the chapters, but the bearing of the fourth can only be gathered from the general trend of his writings. The "Subjective Synthesis" was to have been the crown and completion of his labours.

Until he was forty-four years of age he had been the apostle of truth. The conversion to truth and reality had come to him in early boyhood and he had laboured with unremitting zeal to lay the foundations of the new order on a firm basis of demonstrated truth. He had reviewed and sifted all the abstract sciences man had then acquired and had discovered and taught the science of sociology the necessary prelude to the Religion of Humanity. He stood before the world as the acknowledged exponent of truth. The savants of Europe accepted the positive philosophy as the expression of the co-ordination of scientific reality.

Then he met her who had already discovered, through the difficulties of her own life, the human sanction for right conduct and he became the apostle of goodness, the co-founder with her of the Religion of Humanity, where love, guided by truth, regulated and perfected life, and his " Positive Polity " was written which has been accepted by men of social feeling and synthetic brain as the guide to the Religion of the future.

Dwelling on this union of truth and goodness stimulated his love of beauty, and in his final teaching he drew all things round the central idea of Humanity into one lovely and harmonious whole. The apostle of truth and goodness became the apostle of beauty. True beauty, a harmony of parts, could only be attained by uniting all things by the glow of human love, and this was no arbitrary conception but natural to man when once his eyes were opened to see truth and reality. " The real æsthetic era is still to come ". For the imagination of man must be brought into service as well as his reasoning power and his moral sense, this will help abstract meditation by making images more vivid, the one important proviso being to distinguish imagination from demonstrated truth. If this were clear there would be no danger of the loss of the reality which had been painfully attained through long ages of labour and research.

Although the book was written, as we have seen, in 1856, he supposes himself to be writing in 1927 (in this very year), when he thought the belief in reality would be more firmly established and " many evils and hindrances would be cleared away " and " the leading minds regenerated ". Alas ! the upset of the war seems to have revived old superstitions, and the leading minds do not declare themselves.

He did, however, consider the effect on men of his own day and recognised that practical men trained in science, and doctors, were prepared, in some degree, for the full synthesis.

In the first sentence he sums up in a few words the three aspects, practical, theoretic and moral, of the problem man has to solve would he attain unity : " To subordinate progress to order, analysis to synthesis, egoism to altruism ", these are three aspects of one problem but the last is the source of the solution, " for order presupposes love, and synthesis can only be the result of sympathy ", the object of this work, written for teachers, is to guide universal education to this end. He himself, he says, will only be able to deal with mathematics and morals, the two extremes of the scale, and their application to industry, the intermediate sciences he leaves to his successors. As he had declared that his predecessors, Descartes and Leibnitz, were the founders of positive philosophy in the past, so he acknowledged that the poetic idealisation of the synthesis would be the work of his successors, thus he could venerate the powers of the future as well as the past and recognised his own limitations. There was one principle which could lead to unity in Humanity and that was love, it was subjective and going out from Humanity united us to all things in and through her. Only through Her eyes and according to Her nature could we perceive the world.

That all things may be referred to Humanity the fetichism of Her early days must be united with the positivism of her maturity, for it is the transference of the human feeling of the child and the primitive man to the things around them which makes love all pervading: " Except ye become as little children ye cannot enter the Kingdom of Heaven ", and this is also true of the heaven of the human imagination. The fetichism of childhood and of maturity are both subjective, but the first is absolute and the type is individual, the second relative and the type social. Between these two in the history of the race came the objective or theological explanation which was necesssary but passing. So transferring the social feeling to the Earth we feel that she is loving and we know that she is active, and although it would be confusing to imagine her endowed with intelligence, as her plans might clash with those of Humanity, we can, if we will, imagine her endowed with intelligence in the past consciously preparing herself for the life of Humanity, surrendering thought to her more happily endowed offspring.

Our imaginings must always correspond with reality, that is, we must not imagine things opposed to demonstrated truth. An instance of this would be if we imagined the earth malevolent and inimical to human life, for the fact that the life of Humanity has been developed and perfected through the ages is proof positive that her surroundings have been on the whole beneficial.

The Destiny which was vaguely worshipped in primitive times is summed up for us in the " First Philosophy ", the most abstract and general laws which apply to all things both to the world without and to man's nature, and on which, most fortunately we can build and they bring about in us that " submission " which " is the basis of all improvement ". Relieved from caprice, naturally attaching to the gods, science placed intellectual greatness on an exact submission of the within to the without. The growth of this led to the submission of reason to faith in the last theological religion; this was a sign of the free acceptance of the continuous authority of the past and future over the present. Even enforced submission tends to diminish egoism but by voluntary obedience sympathy is increased. Veneration for an inflexible destiny, because of its moral effect on man, becomes the sign and security for true regeneration. Love embraces the regulations imposed upon us.

Love and worship must then be extended to the world and destiny. While the early worship of destiny was founded on fear the later is founded on love and gratitude. It has been foreshadowed in the East by the worship of the heaven, and in the West by the conception of the universal ether. But both these ideas require to be made subjective for the seat of this destiny is within. That inner space on which Humanity places her abstractions and where alone we find the perfect circle, triangle, or other idealisations of sense impressions. Some dim perception of this truth, that perfection can be found only in the ideal, inspired Plato's conception of all real things being but imperfect copies of the idea in the mind of God. This construction of Comte which has seemed difficult and fantastic to some is not arbitrary but simple truth founded on observation of the working of the human mind. We have all known well the mature fetichism which has endeared the chair where the beloved has sat, and the clothes which have borne the impress, of the form, and of the love which they have been able to renew in our hearts, and the little bit of earth we call our home, how full of love and care it seems to us! As we look at everything from the point of view of Humanity, as our outlook becames more social, we shall feel the inner space which has held Her thought steady and enabled us to comprehend Her past, as worthy of our love and the earth which has supported and made Her life possible as indeed the ancient and beneficient mother which the poets have described; the poets who have held fast to fetichist expressions through the most sceptical ages of man.

We shall understand and feel the reality of the picture Comte draws of each child of man surrounded first by the loving care of Humanity, a threefold circle of family, country and the race, then by the little brothers who by beauty of fur and feather, by helpfulness and friendliness or pretty timidity endear themselves to him, by the lovely circle of trees, plants and flowers which bring shade, food and sweet scents and colours around him, by the circle of the water, pure, sparkling, cleansing and nourishing, by the air which never leaves him, sometimes tender or boisterous, soft and balmy, or keenly invigorating, by our sun, moon and planets, and beyond, by the great background of the Heavens. Love or worship of all these is natural to the human heart. All is summed up in Humanity by whom they are made known to us, this is Her subjective synthesis, Her inward vision by which the many become one. This synthesis conceives all activity as guided by wisdom towards the universal harmony and the intellect receives new consecration and scope, for its aid is needed in connecting the present with the past and the future:

> "Look round our world; behold the chain of Love
> Combining all below and all above."

> "Such is the world's great harmony, that springs
> From order, union, full consent of things:
> Where, small and great, where weak and mighty made
> To save, not suffer, strengthen, not invade;
> More powerful each as needful to the rest
> And, in proportion as it blesses blest;
> Draw to one point and to one centre bring
> Beast, man, or angel, servant, lord or king."
>
> —*Pope.*

Comte had already shewn in the "Polity" the

influence of feeling on thought and the three parts of logic, feeling, images and signs, but adapting it to the subjective synthesis he now altered its definition from the more restricted one " unveiling truths " and extended it to all our powers, the complete definition of logic being: " The normal concert of feelings, images and signs to inspire us with the conceptions which meet our moral, intellectual and physical wants ".

The impulse of the heart alone though strong and deep would be vague and confused without the clear image and the accurate definition. These three methods are connected with the three stages, fetichist, theologic (especially polytheist) and positive, and positivism consecrates all three, bringing into concert strength of feeling, clearness of image and precision of signs ". Intellectual exertion is mainly under the control of the social instincts: " Attachment by arousing attention, Veneration by disciplining it, and Love (Sympathy) by directing it to its true destination ". " Signs and images are to be looked on as the auxiliaries of the feelings in elaborating thoughts ". Signs acquire their chief dignity as alone able to " institute communication between men and Humanity ". Space is the receptacle of all formulas, the earth supplies images, and Humanity is the supreme source of feeling.

Dwelling upon the triumvirate will help us to appreciate submission. Although intellect is centred in Humanity we see Her existence rests on universal love. The earth voluntarily supports Humanity and as the whole existence of space consists of sympathy its submission is complete owing to its passive nature. Thus the soul of the believer feels that the universal order bases improvement on submission. The Human providence is ever subject to order while perfecting it and the result is a noble obedience, for, not being capable of absolute power or of attaining all which She can imagine, the imperfections of Humanity tend to excite progress without recrimination or sense of degradation.

The book then deals with the future teaching of mathematics. All things being referred to Humanity the historic point of view will be kept before the student as well as the dogmatic, and the parts taken by the fetichist, theocratic, Greek and modern peoples made clear. Arithmetic, he points out, is the important part of the calculus, algebra being only a method, the use of the ordinal numbers preceded that of the cardinal as position was required before valuation. He traces the beginning of number before language to the three primaries easily perceived: 1, 2, 3, unity, combination, progression,
unity, order, progress,
a synthesis, a combination, a progression,
Woman, Man, Child.

He emphasises the great step taken in division, the method of approximation, by the theocratic priests over the three fetichist methods and its connection with fractions, the progress of geometry, and its application to astronomy, modern geometry and mechanics. The study of mathematics is a preparation in clearness, precision and consistence but it can only be judged in its relation to the whole. It is the basis of the mental construction of which morals is the aim. Restricted to the base, materialism and dryness result, a perpetual childhood of abstract reason; without the base, social and moral phenomena become incoherent and vague. Mathematics, therefore, must be the basis of all education and, taught historically, it develops veneration, losing the dryness with which it has been accused when studied as an end in itself. Comte suggested the universal use of the septimal scale and upheld it with careful reasoning. Mathematics is the study of space, the seat of abstract phenomena and universal law, but its three divisions, number, extension and movement form a progression directed to Space, the Earth and Humanity, thus the mathematical prepares the universal synthesis and though geometry is logically the most important part, regarded scientifically, mechanics becomes so, as each science and division of science acquires dignity as it rises in the scale and approaches morals.

After dealing fully with mathematics Comte ended the volume by urging the formation of a body of Positivist teachers which was the crying need of the time; and this is even more evident to-day than when he wrote, since the many means of acquiring knowledge, now at the service of all, leads to the mental incoherence he dreaded. How he himself could illuminate the subjects he taught and deprive them of all dryness even when he was only the apostle of truth is shewn by the words of his English pupil Hamilton who writes: "I could not feel, much less measure his greatness but I acquired an interest in the dry science he taught me and had I continued under his charge I might have become a mathematician ", and adds that he was at the time " but dimly conscious of the value of lessons which I can never forget in their higher meaning, though the angles and curves which they explained have long since become to me more meaningless than hieroglyphics ".

CHAPTER XV

KNOW THOU THYSELF ENOUGH FOR MAN TO KNOW

THE work Comte was able to carry out was now finished, for the worn-out body could no longer support the demands of the brain. While he had left to his successors the intermediate volumes of the Subjective Synthesis he had intended himself to write the final and most important volume on morals and also a separate work on industry. Fortunately he had planned the chapters of his work on morals and the names of these combined with indications gleaned from his earlier writings give some idea of the line he would have taken. The work was to have consisted of two parts, the first volume on theoretic morals, that is, the science of individual conduct, the foundation of the general rules which are to guide us, and the second on practical morals, the education proper for each period of life.He had shewn that the science of morals, or of manners, the understanding of ourselves and others, was the highest and might even be called the only science since all the others are but introductory. The old English poet expressed the truth when he said, " Know thou thyself enough for man to know ", for before the nature of man can be fully understood all other truths must have been established. The laws of the earth which condition his existence, of the structure of his body, and of the growth of the society of which he forms a part, lead up to and find their completion in the one fully reasonable and positive study that of the soul of the individual man. The earlier sciences have to do with the conditions and the body of man, the latter with the soul, the soul depends upon the body therefore the sciences which have to do with the earth, the body and the social surroundings of men all form parts of the one sacred science, including all the knowledge it is possible for him to attain. In the former sciences the brain of man was sufficient to construct the scientific basis but in morals the active co-operation of the sexes was necessary. Woman had, from the earliest times, been occupied with practical morals, with the art of life, the understanding of the nature and regulation of the conduct of her children; and man had the habit of scientific observation, of abstraction which was necessary for the formation of general rules. In morals the complete fusion of the masculine and feminine brain was necessary and we cannot understand the work of Comte unless we also understand the part taken by Clotilde in the regeneration of the world, unless we appreciate the humility of the greatest mind Humanity has produced in its recognition of the even greater importance of the heart. These two whom Humanity has joined together let no man put asunder. The "method" in morals is sympathy. It is the subjective method, the highest of all, drawn from within, by our own feelings we feel the joys and sorrows of others. Without this all the knowledge of which we have been speaking would be useless and even harmful but with it the added knowledge becomes of supreme importance, it harmonises our lives and helps us to harmonise the lives of those with whom we are brought in contact, for the saying of old is profoundly true: " Though I have all knowledge and have not charity I am nothing ". In the Introduction Comte would have dealt with all the sciences which are the foundation of the science of man and would have shewn how he could increase, by grateful and loving acceptance, or diminish, by indifference and non-recognition, the beneficial influence of the seven circles on which his life depends and from which he cannot escape. Exactly in proportion to the sympathy he brings to bear upon his surroundings does he derive spiritual benefit from them.

The first chapter was to deal with the " Cerebral Theory ", the equipment by which man acts upon the world and receives its action. On this both the lowest and highest life depend, the vegetable life depends on renewal of substance and this means that the outer world is altered, something is taken out of the surroundings, and the being is also altered as something is taken in and assimilated causing its growth and development. In animal life where the substance required is at a distance the being must have sensibility, the power by which he realises that the outside thing is there, and the power of taking hold of it, he must be able to extend and shorten his muscles to reach distant things and bring them to himself. These two powers lie within the being and, in addition to these, there is something that lies between them, something that acts after the animal has received the impression of the outside object and before he draws it to himself. This " something " consists of the instincts or desires which lie within the animal varying in number with his position in the scale, but in the case of man and the higher animals consisting of all the instincts we find in the table of the soul, from the desire for food, the lowest and most general, to the sympathy which finds its full fruition in the social existence of Humanity. These instincts well up spontaneously from within and lead to the connections between the brain of man and the outside world.

How are these desires or feelings which make the vital spontaneity of the animal, to be themselves disciplined and brought into service, what power is to reach them? Man is ready to modify and improve the world as his powers increase but what is to change the fierce animal who would seize and devour anything which he desires for the moment into that highest product we know, the intelligent humane man or woman regarding the surrounding sevenfold circles with reverence, and desiring the peace, happiness and mutual confidence of all creatures. The second chapter on the *Theory of the Great Being* would have dealt with this question. The one Humanity can itself be divided into a Trinity of circles which gradually surround the individual man and form and save his soul. First comes the Family which takes his lowest and most imperious instincts under its protection and by uniting them to some of his weaker and nobler feelings bind them in service. The instinct of sex and the fierce maternal instinct even in the most rudimentary family bring out tenderness and consideration for others and both unite to modify the entirely selfish or personal desire for food, so irresistible in the lonely undisciplined animal. Then the Tribe or City takes under its protection the furious instinct of destruction, the blind impulse to create, the strong desire to rule, the insidious wish to please, all these the larger social body gradually wins to social service uniting them with admiration of those who have already shewn their strength, their creative power, their ability to rule men, and their winning ways. And, finally, Humanity, revealing the social being who inhabits the whole earth and fill the halls of Time, unites all these feelings in the service of the highest desire natural to man, the instinct of sympathy or benevolence. Nor is it only the inner life of man that is improved and trained by these three beneficient beings, all his senses, his powers of hand and eye are first spontaneously developed in the home, then systematically trained under men of skill in the city, and, finally, all the inventions throughout the world, and in past ages, are brought to his service that his sense power may be indefinitely increased, that the most distant star and the minutest microbe may be visible to his eye, that voices from the remote distance may be heard and the cry for help of the drowning mariner reach the land in time to save, that the smallest change in the temperature of the blood or the slightest crackle of the lung or murmur of the heart may be revealed for the help of the physician, and every power of our senses may be magnified while the irritability and contractility by which the primitive creature perceived food and opened his mouth or stretched out a claw to grasp it becomes the understanding and calculating upon the distant food supplies and the power to send forth trains and ships to distant lands for the things we desire to possess. Thus the social beings re-act on the brains and lives of the beings which compose them and it is evident that would we understand man or know ourselves we must understand the conditions and effect of the composite lives which surround us.

The third chapter, was to be entitled " The Theory of Unity ", Union, Unity, Continuity. All the desires which are found together in the soul of man would lead to agitation and disorder, each one clamouring for its own satisfaction unless they could find a common aim, unless the personal desires could be taught to serve the social and attain harmony and unity, and the individual man is so weak, his life so short, that it is only in the life of Humanity that his life can be continued, that his work can be appreciated and understood and his aims carried out. If his aims have been purely selfish they will fall with his life and be forgotten, only if he has striven for the life of Humanity will he find continuity or immortality. Progress is found by absorption in something higher than self and this is true of the social organisms of which we have been speaking. The family which does not work consciously or unconsciously in the interests of the city, or community of which it forms a part, which pursues its own interests to the detriment of the whole, cannot attain harmony, its very existence will soon be threatened, at any rate its surroundings will soon be suspicious, resentful, hostile; and the country or empire which strives for its own expansion at the expense of others, exploiting the feeble, forgetting the harmony of Humanity, will at last find itself faced with a nemesis and will crumble to the dust. That the individual soul may attain unity and harmony not only he himself but the social beings on whom he depends must recognise and fulfil the law of love. The union between love and truth is never fully attained though we are always approaching it: " Man tends to become more and more religious ". The unchangeable order is necessary outside man but it needs man to explain it, and the laws he observes are more regular than the outside world because they are abstractions, they are an average of the conditions. The universal harmony, in which freedom for each will be found, depends on the effect of lower things on higher as well as the opposite. Unless we all depended on the society around us anarchy would be the result, and if we could not modify the laws of society we should be automata. Progress implies life, the change on the surface of the earth is brought about by the living beings, vegetable and animal, who are constantly modifying it, and progress in

Humanity is brought about by the generations of the living, as one by one they pass by, adding little or much in proportion to the energy and faithfulness of their members. The influence of the past becomes stronger, we learn from it, honouring the outworn beliefs as the best possible at the time, going forward on the same upward path but with a better compass to guide us, a compass we owe to the efforts of those who have gone before. Union then, the coming together under the influence of feeling, has led, and will lead more perfectly, to unity of thought, and this social union with a common aim results in the continuity of man.

The fourth chapter was to be the "Theory of Life": "Existence, Health, Disease". Existence, or life, consists in the action and interaction between the living being and its surroundings; health, or ease, is the condition when this takes place without any friction, when the living being, vegetable or animal, finds in its surroundings all that it requires and is capable of absorbing and turning it to use; disease is the condition when that harmony is broken, either by the failure of the outside condition, or of the being itself. If the want of harmony be carried beyond a certain point death is the result. In disease some part of the body is sluggish and drags behind the other parts, or is feverish and functions too quickly. Health is harmony between the brain and all the other parts of the body. What causes the disturbance of this harmony, where is the root of it? It has two roots, or possible causes, the one lies outside and the other within, and the proportion between these two causes is constantly changing as the animal rises in the scale of being. In the lower forms of life and in the earliest stages of man's existence the cause is generally from without, but in the later life of man in society it is most frequently from within. Man in society is comparatively protected from outside dangers. Food has been stored up to guard against famine, clothes and houses and artificial warmth protect him from the extremes of the climate and floods and tempests, but with civilisation the inner life becomes more complicated, man is a finer instrument and the balance is more easily disturbed; even when the illness comes from without it can be very largely modified by the state of the mind of the patient. Those who attend the patient should remember that they form a part of the outer conditions that may affect him all the more profoundly because of the bonds of sympathy that unite them; calmness and helpfulness may be the determining factor as to his recovery or death. The positivist doctrine recognises both roots of disturbance and while realising the dependence of the mind on the body and on external conditions, it also recognises the power of the mind to re-act on these. Thus positivism avoids the Scylla of materialism which chains the soul to the body and the Charybdis of idealism which gives no anchorage or firm resting-place. Depending as we do on our senses for our communication with the outside, and interaction with the surroundings, it would seem to follow that the man who had all his senses acute and in full working order must be the most successful, and this is true with the savage man surrounded by external dangers, he scents danger from afar and hears and sees in time to secure his safety, but with civilised man the case is different, ill-health or even the loss of a sense sometimes intensifies the inner life and stimulates the sufferer to efforts to overcome his difficulties which carry him in attainment far beyond his fellows. How many cases of this kind there are in the past. Saint Theresa was an invalid, Milton, in his blindness, sang: " so much the more celestial light shine inward ", and in our own day, Henry Fawcett rose above his blindness and lived a life of active public work, Helen Kellar, in what seemed the hopeless condition of blindness and deafness, became an accomplished woman and authoress, and Frederick Walsh, speechless and apparently cut off from all communication, won through and understood, and even attained sainthood in, the religion of Humanity. The harmony between the bodily existence and the mental life is only found when sympathy prevails over selfishness. Very often the source of the illness lies in the affections or desires and the cause is lack of altruism. When the harmony of nations is disturbed and peaceful industry is replaced by fierce passions and war, plague and pestilence follow. This is by no means the result only of the evil outer conditions produced, it is also caused by the fever of the mind, the unrest, the agitation, the fear and hatred engendered, and often in private life when our minds are upset (a condition of disease) some personal feeling has been aroused, we have been slighted or ill-used, or those we love have been wrongly treated and our anger is excited. These feelings upset our bodily organs, we cannot digest our food, our nerves are overstrained and we are predisposed to any illness that may be about. The master tells us " to seek outside ourselves the sources of our actions and conduct ". In Humanity is our health and strength, if we throw ourselves into the stream of her life all our grievances will be washed away, we shall be absorbed in the larger life and some degree of health will be our portion. The fully healthy life can only come when the social conditions are altered. While our fellows are in anxiety for their daily bread, while children perish of starvation we can hardly desire to be ourselves perfectly happy and, therefore, we shall not be altogether healthy, but the more we let the WE prevail over the I, the more we seek the good of others rather than our own selfish gratifications, the more we control our tempers and develop our sympathy, the more nearly shall we attain true health, for he who loses his life shall find it. The influence of the brain on the body when reinforced by the social brain, by the opinions and thoughts of those around, and of men who have lived in the past, becomes very strong and when we come to the influence of Humanity on her own nature and on the world outside we find it impossible to limit it or to say how much more may be attained.

The three last chapters were to deal with "Feeling, Intelligence and Activity ". The fifth on Feeling is divided into " Personality, Sociality and Morality ". The personal and the social instincts are both necessary and in their varied combinations form the differing characters which make a combined social life possible. Every variety of normal human being is necessary to fit into the different requirements of Humanity, the love of power, of approbation, or even of destruction can be enlisted in social service; he in whom the destructive instinct is strong may become the pioneer, to clear away either the primeval forest or the modern social evil, while one who loves construction can build the log hut, or plan the new social order. He who loves power may marshal his fellows in service, and he who desires praise may win them to it, and the varying degrees of love, reverence and pity are so great that we lose ourselves in trying to see the endless variety. It is this personality or individuality that we love in our friends and which makes it impossible that one should ever take the place of another. Each man should have the work especially adapted to his powers and idiosyncrasy, and with the education of every child in the meaning of Humanity little more will be needed to control the strong natures and make them see that the true path to success is in turning their exceptional powers to the service of the whole. When the personal part of our nature serves the social then we have attained morality, the harmony of life.

The title of the sixth chapter was to be " Theory of the Intelligence ", " *Abstract Reason, Concrete Reason, Mental Harmony*". There are two kinds of reason which must work together if mental harmony is to be the result. The one is the power of abstract reasoning, of perceiving the general truths which lie within and behind all passing events, the other is the power of dealing with the problems of the moment and deciding wisely and quickly. In the thoroughly capable man or woman these two are combined, but they are often separated and one man is much occupied with abstract truth but is not capable of dealing with the problems of daily life, while another is so occupied with daily life that he does not trouble about general truths at all. An extreme example of the first is that of Ampère who is said to have been so occupied with his problem that he wrote it on the back of a cab thinking it was a blackboard and when the cab moved on ran with it without noticing that the cab was moving. The average Englishman is generally supposed to represent the other type being entirely occupied with practical work. In the life of Humanity mental harmony is found when the intellectual and practical men work together, the practical acknowledging and submitting to the supremacy of the abstract or general laws and the intellectual man allowing complete freedom to the practical in carrying out the work of daily life.

The harmony of feeling being attained by love drawing self into service and of thought by the balance of abstract thought with that relating to the immediate problems before us, the harmony of action will follow naturally, and the seventh chapter was to be called: "Theory of the Activity: Practical, Philosophic, Poetic". Man's action takes three differing forms: first, the *practical*, which is generally called "action", because it deals with the actual things around us, moulding them to the use of man; second, the *philosophic*, by which man strives to unite things into one coherent whole, to find the general laws underlying all passing events; and third, the poetic, which idealises both thought and action and raises the whole of life to a higher level of beauty. The more these three are united the more complete the individual, the more satisfactory his life. The practical man should enter into the wider meaning of which his work forms part, and should idealise that work, and the relationships of daily life. The philosopher should understand and share in practical life and in its idealisation, and the poet should so comprehend practical life and thought that his idealisations may be on the lines of possible progress. There is one kind of work in which all three must be combined and which is therefore the best symbol or type of the life of Humanity. It is that of the mother. If she is to succeed in her task of the making of men and in women she must be practical, that she may train her children in order and punctuality, in precision and accuracy so necessary in practical work, scientific investigation or artistic construction. She must not be only practical or she will cramp and starve the higher aspirations of the future. She needs a philosophic outlook which connects her with the larger life of the world, not only with the active life of the generation in which she lives but with the past and with the future, with the life of Humanity. Last, but not least, she needs the poetic or ideal view of life that she may help her children to rise from the details of daily life and physical necessities

> "Above the smoke and stir of this dim spot
> Which men call Earth".

The three forms of activity are all necessary in the life of the world, they are three parts of the one thing, the synergy or united action which is the result of socialised feeling united to harmonised thought. For philosophy brings the efforts of the present into line with the past, and poetry shews the possibilities of development in the future, and practice plods along towards it. This union of the three would make life beautiful with very little external change, for it is the inner life which glorifies the outer.

The heading of the conclusion of the theory of morals is "Synthesis, Sympathy, Religion". In order to arrive at the best kind of conduct, at the practical morals which is the aim and crown of the whole life work of the master, in order that every child of man may have the best kind of education from the cradle to the grave, these three are necessary; Synthesis, unity of thought, summed up in the one centre, dedicated to one purpose. This "thought unity" can only be formed within through comprehension of the life of Humanity. For if we try to centralise our thoughts on any outside power we have two centres, our thoughts turn to Humanity even while we are striving to concentrate them on God or Nature. Only such men as the hermits of the middle ages or some eastern mystics could attain a synthesis outside Humanity, and how precarious it was! always liable to be upset by recrudescence of human feelings. In the synthesis of Humanity the will is not imposed from without but grows from within, it is not superior to labour regarding it as a curse but recognises it as one of the greatest blessings, by humble patient labour Humanity has conquered the earth and through it man has ascended the ladder of life. All things are made one for us in and by the mind of Humanity and we have no other way to learn save through Her mind without us, or using our portion of Her mind within. The object of synthesis, or unity of thought, is that all may be brought within the realm of sympathy. "The heart of man cannot conceive" how rapid the change would be in the whole conditions of life if once the method of sympathy prevailed. Love easily blends with love, goodness with goodness. St. Thomas tells us it is difficult to live with hard and perverse persons but only love can overcome hate and goodness evil, and sympathetic understanding should meet every case. Three voices were raised soon after the rebirth of the French Revolution to express the desire that love should reach the evil as well as the good. Wordsworth, speaking of the man who communed with nature and entered into the aspirations of Humanity, says:

"He looks around
And seeks for good and finds the good he seeks
Until abhorrence and contempt are things
He only knows by name and if he hear
From other mouths the language which they speak
He is compassionate and has no thought,
No feeling which can overcome his love."

And Shelley makes Prometheus, the embodiment of progress, cry when he foresees the downfall of Jupiter the tyrant:

> "Disdain? Ah, no, I pity thee,
> I speak in grief
> Not exultation for I hate no more
> As then ere misery made me wise."

And the third is the voice to which we delight to listen, that of Clotilde de Vaux as she says:

> "The wicked are more in need of pity than the good."

Thus thought uniting all, and the highest social instinct being the method of our dealing with each other, and with the earth and her surroundings, Religion will be attained, there will be harmony, our minds will reflect the external world well and truly, our love will unite all things within. If these things look utopian we have only to look back to see how the utopias of the past have become realities of the present, and wherever a utopia has constantly recurred we may be sure that even if it be never attained the course of Humanity will be towards it. This makes us sure that the ideal of peace will be realised and the nations will live in unity in Her, nay, that there will be peace between man and the higher animals, for how often that desire has been in the heart of Humanity, that utopia in her imagination. The biological league which Comte predicted has been foreshadowed again and again never more beautifully than in the Hebrew Scriptures:

> "The wolf also shall dwell with the lamb, and the leopard shall lie down with the kid, and the calf and the young lion and the fatling together; and a little child shall lead them—",

Fetichism and positivism united, Humanity leading while her heart has become as that of a little child. The beautiful utopias of the race will mould mankind in their likeness, they are the ideals Humanity creates that she may attain them. The utopia of the Eucharist, that each believer partaking of the actual body of the God would grow in his likeness, had a profound effect in Europe in the middle ages. The advance of man may be traced in the perfecting of the utopias through the ages as shewn in Religion. There has been a constantly recurring utopia connected with woman beginning in very early times when many coarse rites performed by her were still continuing (these rites themselves being connected with her function of motherhood in which the highest attribute of Humanity, her continuity, is founded). This utopia is the realisation of purity and tenderness, the qualities of the maiden and of the mother, symbolised by the lily and the rose, the dove and the pelican, and in many other ways. In the Greek days these qualities were separated and were the attributes of different goddesses, Pallas Athena and Aphrodite. Pallas Athena, whose birth was an immaculate conception, was the goddess of wisdom and purity, but tenderness was not her attribute. In the middle ages both qualities were united in the Madonna whose birth was also immaculate but her highest attribute was purity. In Humanity tenderness and purity are again combined but of all human attributes tenderness is the highest. Thus does the Religion of Humanity put forward the highest ideal to guide all relations of life. Attained completely we can never hope to see it but it will be more and more nearly attained as the generations pass, each one bringing its tribute to the greatest of all creations the creation and development of the life of Humanity.

CHAPTER XVI

THE INHABITANT

> "Shall I stay captive i' the outer Court
> Surprised with that, and not advance to know
> Who dwells there and inhabiteth the house?"
>
> —BEN JONSON.

THE whole work of Comte, the Foundation, the Main Building and the Superstructure had but one object, the shelter of the soul; that man and woman might realise the dignity of the human destiny and feeling themselves a part of a larger life might be saved from loneliness, from isolation and from

> "the miserable aims that end with self."

The volume on Practical Morals may be summed up in one word: Education, education which has a series of steps proper to each phase of life beginning with conception and ending only with death. The passage of the soul from the past to the future would then be a continuous development, the treasure handed on by those who have gone before would be guarded and increased for the benefit of those who come after.

Mutual love, Clotilde had pointed out, was a

necessity for successful marriage, and the pair thus prepared for parenthood, and feeling its supreme importance in the life of Humanity would begin the education of the child from conception. As the body of the mother is guarded from harm so her mind should be guarded from evil and from petty or sordid feelings. She is creating the mind and body of the child and whether she will or no must influence his destiny; all who are brought in contact with her should help her in this task. The child should be received into a world of love, should hear no harsh words and feel no ungentle touch; during infancy his love has to be brought out to all around him, to people, animals and things. At this period attachment is developed which gives him certainty and tenacity in after-life; now too he must learn obedience that later he may take his part in ordered service.

As he passes from infancy to childhood, when his powers of hand and eye are growing, he should see and hear beautiful things. At this period his taste is formed, and the ideals set before him should be worthy of imitation. As he passes from childhood to youth and his powers of mind increase he must learn the art of reasoning, must be "initiated" in the methods of the sciences, in deduction, observation, experiment, definition, comparison and in history and morals. Having received training in love, in beauty and in truth, he will be of age, and be able himself to understand the doctrine of Humanity and to enter Her service. A woman, having received the same education, will generally soon after this time become herself the centre of a family, and will be prepared by motherhood to exercise her threefold function, moral, spiritual and temporal: " To warn, to comfort, to command ", but a man will for some time make trials of skill, testing his powers until he has finally decided on his work in life, he will then be dedicated, consecrated to the service of Humanity that he may not strive for his own hand alone, or exploit or overreach his fellows, but, whatever his work may be, do it for the benefit of all. He will strive to perfect himself in that work and will learn veneration for the masters of his craft in the past and in the present, for the fathers of the city and for noble ideals. This veneration will steady his action and make him a mature man, one whose judgment can be relied on in adversity and prosperity. He will have formed a family and adapted his strength to the needs of those weaker than himself. He will learn his double duty as expressed in the master's words:

> " In the normal order every man ought continually to reconcile two different occupations, on the one hand his special labours, on the other hand his just solicitude with respect to the general economy. Social harmony would be as much compromised by the habitual abandonment of great public interests as by chronic neglect of real private duties ".

Having exercised his powers to the full he will find

he has another lesson to learn, he has to be educated for a further advance.

Leaving the active work to younger men his function will be advisory. His advice must be ready for his successors. It will also be sought on general matters, for no longer having to struggle in active life he will have a more tolerant outlook, his long experience of life will have helped him to understand difficulties and temptations, and sympathy and goodwill to all should become his leading characteristics. This harmony and goodwill will gradually prepare him to pass into the subjective life where he will become an influence for good, and will help to build up the ideal which is to inspire the children of the future. By " seeking not his own " he will have entered into the larger life and will have found a satisfaction and joy that selfish aims can never give; all the sides of his nature developed his education will be complete.

CHAPTER XVII

The Passing

"I see in you the estuary that enlarges and spreads itself grandly as it pours in the great sea."

—Walt Whitman.

THE eleven years from Clotilde's death until he himself passed into the subjective life were years of steady progress towards perfection. He gradually disciplined his life both physical and intellectual. He took two meals a day, the first principally of milk, the other more solid, at the end of which he was accustomed to eat a piece of bread slowly, thinking of all those who could only obtain this simple food with difficulty, of the masses whose suffering had inspired his life's work. Coffee, tobacco and wine he had given up and now he abstained from second-rate reading, dwelling more and more with the masterpieces of the race. Every year he re-read Homer, Dante and St. Thomas a Kempis. He rose at five and went to bed at ten, spending the first and last hour in prayer, filling his mind in the morning with the image of his beloved, and, in the evening, bringing every thought and action of the day before her, comparing them with the standard her example and nature had set up in his soul. Thus he attained more and more complete mastery over himself and could foresee when a long and difficult work would be finished ; he transformed his ardent, suspicious and impatient disposition until it became calm and gentle, sunny and long suffering like the ideal in his heart. " I have reduced ", he says, " the discipline of human nature to the constant culture, direct and indirect, of the sympathetic instincts as the source of duty, of happiness and of health ". " His manner ", says one of his English disciples, " was that of the old school of French gentlemen; simply dressed, not striking in bodily presence, he possessed much natural dignity ". " He was kindly and at some times even playful and did not obtrude his opinions ".

From 1851, when many of those who did not care for religious reconstruction fell away from him, the Positivist Society became like one family with friendly intercourse between its members united by their admiration of the master, who helped them to reform old habits and avoid old errors. He made a choice of books, The Positivist Library of the Nineteenth Century, which contains intellectual treasures in poetry, science, history, religion and philosophy, which he advised them to read in place of the many futile publications in common use. All his mental and moral powers were shewn in the sacraments he conferred, and those who took part in them felt an emotion the memory of which was never lost. " Religion ", said one who was present, opened the treasures of her grace and showered upon her children her most precious gifts: peace, concentration of mind, love, faith, charity ". Many of his followers regarded the years in which they were privileged to know him as the happiest of their lives. They looked forward to the Wednesday evenings when the meetings were held, and as each large volume of the " Polity " was published devoured it eagerly. He was deeply convinced of the intimate connection between right thinking and right conduct, and his object was to form a body of men and women who should make the religion of Humanity the inspiration of their thought and the guide of their lives.

Sophie's constant protecting care led to her adoption as his daughter, and to the reception of her husband and children into his home, thus the alliance between the philosopher and the people, which he preached, was fulfilled in his own experience. For the first time since his childhood he tasted the peace and happiness of domestic life and drew from it deep draughts of inspiration. Clotilde and Sophie became sisters in his heart, his two adopted daughters; for his worship and meditations had convinced him that he would have carried out his resolution made before her death of adopting Clotilde as his daughter, even though he had learned she loved him; they could not have gone back from the ideal relation to which they were called by social duty. He had formulated the duty of the partners in an unhappy marriage. The duty of the husband was a monetary one, he must support the wife. Both might seek consolation in a happier connection but it must remain a connection of heart and mind alone. He rejoiced that in spite of the isolation of his life he had been blessed by the devoted love of three noble women, Rosalie, Clotilde and Sophie.

In 1852 he met Captain Marie at Clotilde's tomb who clasped his hand expressing gratitude for Comte's continued worship of her, and after that Comte associated her father with her, remembering that meeting and how he had visited him after her death and had requested that the MS. of " Wilhelmine " should be given to him.

On the first day of every year he was cheered by messages or visits from his disciples.

But even in these happiest years of his life he had many trials and difficulties, he was " a man of sorrows ", as are all who strive to bear the burdens of others and open a path of progress. He was struggling with poverty and says, sadly, that while those working for regeneration need not fear now for life and liberty, as in the days of old, yet material oppression demands a deeper and more continuous resignation. When engaged on his " Polity " he was able to put the thought of this aside but when that was concluded in 1854 it caused him serious anxiety, especially for two reasons, one that he feared he should be unable to pay the annuity to his wife, and the other that he should have to give up the apartment so precious to him because there his Vita Nuova had begun.

The more nearly his finely sensitive temperament approached a normal condition of calm the more profoundly was it shaken by any want of harmony but when this happened he strove at once to recover his equilibrium by turning again to his ideal. His weekly visit to the church of St. Paul inspired him with more sympathy for catholicism, it led to his final reconciliation with his father and sister and suggested the religious league to his mind. Speaking of his volume on history, he said:

> " This incomparable voyage through the entire range of human history will facilitate all my future labours by making me feel the influence of the past more deeply. Catholicism had thrown off the Greco-Roman past, protestantism rejected the Middle Ages, and deism threw off all continuity. Positivism accepts the whole past as the gradual development of the one religion. Every political upset is a hindrance to religious reorganisation, only a return to calm can lead to progress and the disturbance of foreign relations is incompatible with aspirations after a better order. The true solution of social questions is religious ".
>
> " Positivism restates the programme sketched by the Middle Age. To regulate public and private life by placing intellect under the guidance of feeling. The anarchy of the West first affected international relations and it is upon these that the new spiritual power should begin to assert its influence. The first object of the reorganisation is to reawaken in the weak veneration for the strong by an exceptional devotion of the strong to the weak ".

During the conception of each of his principal works Comte's fine organisation subjected him to a physical crisis. The milieu of the Revolution and the fatalities of his own career were not favourable to his central equilibrium. The " Philosophy ", united to his domestic trials, brought the terrible crisis of 1826; the " Polity ", a long period of fever ending in erysipelas, the " Subjective Synthesis " was preceded by a nervous crisis and his meditation on morals added to two painful shocks which he experienced, was more than his weakened body could bear and resulted in his death.

In April, 1857, his friend, the statesman Viellard, became ill. He had watched Comte's career sympathetically from the first, had intervened more than once in his favour with the authorities and had said, speaking of the " Positive Philosophy " in 1848, " However blind those in power may be I cannot believe that they really wish to stop the only discipline which can touch the hearts and minds of the people to-day ". Comte visited him in his illness and the bond between them was drawn closer. Almost immediately afterwards Viellard died, having left directions that his body should be buried in the common grave without any religious service. This was a double shock to Comte, who probably hoped he would have publicly declared his acceptance of the Religion of Humanity.

In addition to the shock he, misdirected, and hurrying to the funeral, was caught in a storm and took a severe chill. He became very ill, but by strict regimen, with the care of Sophie, began to recover when a disappointment with regard to one of his young disciples whom he had regarded with warm affection came as a second blow. His emotion was followed by a return of fever and prostration. He again rallied and resumed his correspondence and interviews. In July he passed through a time of great suffering borne with patience and strength of soul. He wished to live especially that he might write his book on morals and find and install his successor. His strength of will kept him alive for some time and, in the presence of death, his intellectual vigour and moral serenity were unimpaired. Dr. Robinet attended him and, on the 31st, Auguste Comte asked him for his opinion on his condition. Robinet's courage failed him, but that evening he wrote telling him that his condition was desperate. The next morning Comte spoke of the letter and reproached Robinet for his weakness saying he had done all he could to preserve his life and had made all arrangements in case of his death and therefore there was nothing to be done but wait calmly to see what the end would be:

> "Then leaving the present his conversation turned to his hopes for the future. He spoke of the work he had done and the plans he had made to hasten the advent of positivism. Then abandoning himself to the usual ardour of his friendly outpourings he turned the conversation to the highest regions of religious action, contemplating our regenerated descendants enjoying all his genius had conceived for the grandeur

> and improvement of man. Such as I had seen him in his greatest days at the time of his public lectures at the Palais Cardinal, with all the fire of the noblest aspirations, such I saw him now. The ardour and majesty of his soul illumined his face, transforming his features and his voice. Instead of a dying man I had the Founder of Positivism before me as full of grandeur and of strength as I had ever known him. With an overpowering sentiment of enthusiasm and of sorrow, of confidence and of despair, I reverently kissed his wasted hands. It was the last time I was to hear his voice ". (" The Life and Works of Auguste Comte ".)
> *Robinet.*

On the evening of the 4th September he became worse and Madame Thomas wished to send for Dr. Robinet but Comte desired her to wait until the morning. His heart full of the past, meditating on his beloved friend, his hopes, as we have seen, ardently fixed on the future he was not oblivious of the present, he thought of his children, as he called them, of Sophie and her husband who had long watched over him, he had compassion on their weariness and begged, nay almost commanded, them to go to rest. They obeyed him so far as to leave the room but only to watch outside the door for they knew he was not fit to be left alone. The end was, indeed, very near, he sank into unconsciousness but before he passed into eternal silence one sign of life there was. He opened his eyes and fixed them with a look of love and gratitude on the flowers Clotilde had made and given him and then the brain of "The Thinker", the modern "Master of those that know" was at rest and the heart of the Lover of mankind ceased to beat. The earnest desire of this noble and tender heart that he and the three he loved to think of as his guardian angels should be united in one grave could not be realised, and his disciples laid him in Père la Chaise not far from the resting-place of Clotilde, on a spot he had chosen himself near the grave of Elise Mercoeur the poetess.

Oh suffering race of Man, your lonely plight
Inspired my youth to seek and find the way
To loftier realms, where Love might sweetly sway
Your thoughts and lives ; could you but scale the height !
Through toilsome years I strove with zeal and might
To hew the path through which salvation lay,
By steepest rocks to realms of glorious day ;
Then, wearied, paused, the end not yet in sight.

Borne on strong wings of Love, One swiftly passed
And reached the height for which I strove in vain,
She beckoning turned and on me, wearied, cast
A gracious smile which nerved me to attain.
Now, from the height, the lovely plain we scan
Where Heaven on Earth is found, the home of Man.

CHAPTER XVIII

After Days

"Per letiziar lassù folgor s'acquista."

—Paradiso IX.

BEFORE Comte died he felt that the religion of Humanity had been proclaimed to the world, and believed that fervent disciples would be found to preach and perfect it. How has his prophecy been fulfilled in the years since his death? As to the date of its systematic acceptance it has certainly failed, but the ablest seaman, while he can tell the date at which a ship should reach its destination, cannot tell what tempests, head winds, undercurrents or other causes may delay the voyage. Had Comte himself lived longer he might have influenced the rapidity of the change, for his voice was beginning to be heard in many lands, the last work he had planned, his volume on Industry, would have appealed to leading practical men, and his followers would have profited by his direct guidance, for Comte was the truly modern man, the embodiment of the new age in which the social outlook is consciously attained and dominates the whole of life. He was the modern man while we grope and stumble towards modernity, our mental make-up resembling that of a snake whose parched and dried skin has parted shewing a little of the beauty and promise of the future while all the rest is dim, dusty and outworn. France seems to have sold her birthright and abandoned any attempt at religious construction, probably the disturbance which led to the Franco-Prussian war and the bitter resentment which was its consequence, delayed her development though Gambetta was Comte's follower, and the cultured Parisian, who may be of any class and is frequently a workman, has still the most central outlook among the sons of Humanity. Faithful apostles in many lands have not been lacking. As Comte foresaw, the most devoted have been found in the Portuguese and Spanish settlements in South America. In Brazil the Republic was peacefully established under the leadership of Benjamin Constant, an avowed Positivist, the motto " Order and Progress " being chosen for the national flag, while in public affairs the positivists have exercised a marked influence. They have instituted the public celebration of many historic types and the last act of Senhor Mendes, their revered leader, was connected with the statue of St. Francis of Assissi to be erected in Rio. In the older civilisations their voices have been more drowned but in England they have faithfully proclaimed the doctrine with regard to Gibraltar, India, Egypt, Ireland, China, Trades Unions and other matters, while much of the improvement in Poor Law administration, sanitation and the general care of health is due to the strenuous labours of Dr. Bridges, one of Comte's followers who " renounced private practice to devote himself to public work ". In Liverpool a Temple of Humanity has been erected of which the beauty and dignified simplicity is recognised across the Atlantic.

Small indeed have been the conscious and systematic results compared with what might have been, but only seventy years have elapsed since the premature death of Comte, and, it must be remembered, he continually emphasised the fact that there are two ways in which the religion of Humanity may come. The one, the conscious and systematic of which we have spoken, that is, by the acceptance of the doctrine and the attempt to put it into practice, the other, the spontaneous and unconscious, by the gradual dissolving of the old and formation of the new order. " All men are ", he says, " especially in the present day, spontaneous positivists at different stages of evolution which only need completeness ".

To those who have had the privilege of observing society for over half a century, with the enlightening help of the doctrine of Humanity, the change in this respect has been very marked in all spheres of thought and activity. Much careful scientific observation has been carried on, notably in anthropology. Royalty is everywhere passing away, hereditary titles are losing their glamour, dictators tend to arise, and in the country which Comte thought would be second in the acceptance of the religion of Humanity a dictator has arisen from the people who has tried to introduce order into a disorganised society and to foster habits of discipline and devotion to work, unfortunately he has not fulfilled the indispensable condition of allowing spiritual liberty and freedom of speech, and rather resembles a dictator of the past than of the future a position which must inevitably lead to reaction. Turning to our own country, although the ruling classes have not risen, as Comte hoped, to the realisation of the grandeur of the work of accomplishing re-organisation without revolution and have lately, e.g. in the struggle over miners' wages, been engaged in delaying the incorporation of all workmen into society, still, much has been gained. Beautiful parks with costly and rare flowers are secured and tended for the enjoyment of the poorest citizens. Public playgrounds with appliances, far better than those provided for the wealthy fifty years ago, are ready for the little ones. Games, dancing and the arts which teach control and grace of body are doing away with the class consciousness so evident a short time ago, the wives and daughters of the workmen can scarcely be distinguished in the streets from their wealthier sisters. Suffering enough remains, but the dissolving process has begun, class distinction is passing away and the one Humanity is being realised. Cruel and revolting doctrines are preached and forgotten such as "the destruction of the old and diseased", 'compulsory birth control', and through it all devoted doctors are striving with all their skill to save and succour the diseased, and nurses are sacrificing their health and their careers to keep those alive who have lost all but life. Miners instead of securing their own safety are going into the burning pit to lose their lives in the effort to save their fellows. Everywhere men and women are realising that improvement depends on self control and on the gradual advance of the whole, that acts of cruelty and tyranny defeat themselves by lowering the general standard of feeling. Consideration for animals has increased as shown by the Bird Sanctuaries, and such institutions as the Horse processions are a foretaste of the "Festival of the Animals", when the lesser brethren will be honoured in the Temple of Humanity. The improvement in Poor Law Infirmaries, which now compare favourably with the best, the care of children brought up by the State, old age pensions, the humane treatment of prisoners, the diminution of the desire for vengeance by punishment, all point to the growth of social feeling and recognition of social duty. Such a saying as "A man may do what he likes with his own", prevalent fifty years ago, would hardly be asserted now even by the men who still act upon it. Such a saying as "My country right or wrong", once considered rather fine, and certainly a necessity for the soldier in the execution of his duty, is now discredited, and one of the most significant signs of the times is, that, whenever a country is acting tyrannically to a weaker, or exploiting a less advanced race, champions of the oppressed are sure to arise in the oppressing country, who, shewing themselves true patriots oppose her wrong-doing and dishonour. International feeling has grown among the mass of the people in all countries. Men are beginning to realise that as no family can work worthily or gain honour save in the service of city or country so no country can find its fulfilment save as a part of the one whole to which all belong. The League of Nations is one sign of this change and the Assembly of the League is an attempt at an advising or spiritual power resembling in some respects the International Council proposed by Comte.

An extraordinary change has taken place in the doctrines of theology, little acknowledged but none the less vital. The popular novelists have scarcely a ıag of theological belief left, yet people who consider themselves orthodox read, admire and applaud. It sometimes seems as if we needed the little child to say, as in the fairy tale of the King's beautiful garment: " Why he has nothing on ". The very dignitaries of the Church have long given up belief in doctrines such as that of the resurrection of the body, still included in the services and creeds. Quite recently a bishop had the courage to acknowledge that the belief in hell was past, though when he put forward the positive doctrine that the fear of injuring others should be a sufficient deterrent from sin, he did not add that the belief in heaven must also pass away for if the bad did not need punishment surely the good would not need reward. One curious anomaly is seen in the religious teaching of the day. Many preachers have thrown aside the magnificent conception of supreme sacrifice in Christ Jesus, who left the glories of Heaven to suffer for man on earth, but have attempted to retain in the individual man

Jesus all the qualities which have grown up around the ideal type through the Christian era. Even the finest individual type is not enough. It may suffice for private worship, for here the worshipper is nearly always of the opposite sex and the heart of the worshipper becomes a combination of masculine and feminine attributes, but in the public worship the symbol must combine the virtues, thoughts and powers of all mankind. The energy and wisdom of man, the tenderness and wisdom of woman, the widely differing forms of excellence of both, exhibited in every relation and accident of life can be found in no individual man or woman . To imagine them in one must result in the unreality which it is the aim of the modern man to avoid. In the God ideal this mixture was more permissible but the tendency was to monstrosity. This was largely overcome in the Christian dogma by the conception of the Trinity but its inadequacy was felt by Saint Bernard who added the Madonna to introduce the more strictly feminine element. In ' Humanity ' all types are of necessity combined. Goodwill is growing everywhere but with confused thought. Phrases are used without attention to the meaning of words or, at any rate, of their implication. The phrase " Science and Religion are reconciled ", a truth which Comte's life and work have triumphantly proved to the extent that religion can only embrace the whole of life when it is firmly founded on science carried into the highest regions, this phrase, loosely used, makes the ordinary hearer believe that there has been some discovery proving the existence of God, or, in other words, that Science and Theology are reconciled, a very different proposition and totally untrue. They are different ways of accounting for things and can only be reconciled as different phases in the history of Humanity. As in Comte's day, the mental plan is not clear, men have but a confused idea that the industrial era is the ideal of the future while they constantly turn back to the military ideal of the past. We have a vision of the promised land of peace and industry founded on human truth and love but, like the Israelites in the old legend, many turn back to the golden calf of superstition, militarism or of hereditary privilege. While the superstitious belief in science as an end in itself, which was so marked in the 19th century, has passed away few have recognised that the solution is found in science taking service under love while many have returned to more primitive superstitions. Men like Sir James Mackenzie have striven to free the people from the medical tyranny which results from applying the general rule to the particular case using the deductive method in an art which especially calls for careful observation; everywhere men of exceptional insight are adopting the positive method in isolated cases but the mental chaos remains. This mental attitude is, in default of the complete acceptance of the new order, a matter of congratulation as under it the dissolving process is carried on. The new Liverpool Cathedral, situate on a hill not much more than a stone's throw from the Temple for the conscious worship of Humanity, is a place for spontaneous human worship, the noble lives of humble women are recorded in the windows, its bishop strives to draw into one fellowship the different sects of theology, and, by special services for railwaymen and others, begins the festivals of the transition.

The ground of confidence lies in the law of human progress " Man ever grows more religious ", discovered by Comte. This is difficult to see because the meaning of religious is not understood. Men compare the modern world with the theocracies and with the Middle Age and think that religion is dying out, and even comparing the present with a generation or two ago, the discipline of life and recognition of religious duty seems passing away. But religion as Comte defines it, consists of harmony within and without, peace in the mind and union with our fellows. Harmony is the result of the increase of social, and the greater control of personal, feelings. This results from living together. Modern industry depends in a constantly increasing degree on mutual trust, there is less room for suspicion and resentment. As men from different classes and lands associate together and find in all the same kindly feelings, the same aspirations, a sense of security and confidence grows up. As in a happy family the atmosphere is one of fearlessness, wit, humour, joyousness and all the sweet flowers of human intercourse grow apace, so, as the same confidence finds its place in the larger life, as each one feels that his fellows will stand by him in misfortune and share with him in need, joyousness will be the mark of the religious man. It is worthy of notice that the two most widely beloved saints in the Catholic Church, St. Francis and St. Catherine, were distinguished by their gaiety of heart. This gaiety is not that of mere exhuberance of youth, which may be accompanied by much selfishness and lead to a sombre and discontented age, it is the supreme joy of life which results when duty and happiness are one. It is a harmony of heart and this can only be fully attained when there is also a harmony of mind, when feeling, thought and action all tend to one centre. The spontaneous growth of religion can be clearly seen around us and the day is not distant when men will see in whom they have believed and will delight to render honour where honour is due. When that time shall come, as one of our novelists has said, the name of Auguste Comte must arise into prominence. And when the light of Comte's memory rises on the human horizon it will be accompanied by that of the mother who first " by her love his love awoke ", by that of the fair and delicate spirit who by one short year of companionship glorified the whole of his after life and by that of the simple noble hearted woman who loved and tended him to the end.

WORKS OF AUGUSTE COMTE

	Published in
Cours de Philosophie Positive, 6 tomes	1829-1844
Catéchisme Positiviste - - -	1852
Système de Politique Positive, 4 tomes	1851-1854
Circulaires annuelles - - -	1850-1854
Synthèse Subjective - - - - -	1856
Appel aux Conservateurs - - -	1855
Testament, Prières, Confessions et Correspondance avec Clotilde de Vaux - - - - - -	1884
Lettres à M. Valat - - - - -	1870
Lettres à John Stuart Mill - - -	1877
Lettres à Divers, 3 tomes - - -	1902-1905
Correspondance inédite, 4 tomes - -	1903-1904
Lettres et Fragments de lettres - -	1927

OTHER BOOKS CONSULTED

Notice sur l'œuvre et sur la Vie d'Auguste Comte par le Docteur Robinet, 2e édition - - -	1864
Notice sur la Vie et l'œuvre d'Auguste Comte par J. Longchampt - -	1900
L'Amoureuse Histoire d'Auguste Comte et de Clotilde de Vaux par Charles de Rouvre - - - - - -	1917
Religion de l'Humanité, Clotilde et Comte par R. Teixeira Mendes, 4 tomes - - - - - -	1914-1918

Printed in the United States
by Baker & Taylor Publisher Services